ALICE PATTERSON

BRIDGING THE
RACIAL &
POLITICAL
DIVIDE

HOW GODLY POLITICS CAN
TRANSFORM A NATION

TRANSFORMATIONAL PUBLICATIONS

Cover design: Steve Fryer (www.stevefryer.com)
Internal design: David Sluka

BRIDGING THE RACIAL & POLITICAL DIVIDE: HOW GODLY POLITICS CAN TRANSFORM A NATION

Alice Patterson
Justice at the Gate
PO Box 681148, San Antonio, TX 78268
www.justiceatthegate.org
Tel. 210-677-8214

ISBN 10: 0-9752823-9-5
ISBN-13: 978-0-9752823-9-7

Published by Transformational Publications
A division of Harvest Evangelism, Inc.
PO Box 20310, San Jose, CA 95160-0310
Tel. (408) 927-9052
www.harvestevan.org
www.transformourworld.org

Printed in the United States of America

ENDORSEMENTS

WHEN GOD LOOKED AND SOUGHT FOR SOMEONE to stand in America's political gap, we are so fortunate that He found Alice Patterson! There isn't a person in America that understands race, politics and God's heart for reconciliation like Alice does. As you read this book, the scriptures will come alive, and God's love and desire for unity will invade your heart. Unto that end, this book is part of God's history of faithfulness through an incredible intercessor. For many of you, this book will be a watershed moment that will mark you for life.

William Ford III
Hilkiah Ministries, Fort Worth, Texas
Author, *Created for Influence*; **Co author,** *History Makers*

IN A HOUR THAT GOD IS CALLING HIS CHURCH to prayer and civic engagement like never before, Alice, one of God's seasoned veterans in the governmental arena, captures the heart of God for true societal transformation. This book could not have come at a better time and should be required reading for those God is calling to advance His Kingdom in the civic arena. I know God will use Alice, through the revelation in this book, to impact your life, as she has mine.

Mark Gonzales
United States Hispanic Prayer & Action Network, Dallas, Texas

AT LAST, A BOOK THAT UNCOVERS THE SPIRITUAL REALITIES of how politics works. Alice Patterson provides principles for healing the racial and political divides that we must address for real change in America.

Laurraine Huffman
Target 7 Ministries
El Paso, Texas

NO WHERE IN THIS COUNTRY among the 568 tribes of Indians have we ever had a document as clear as *Bridging the Racial and Political Divide*. I've wondered for many years if any book would hit the streets with so vital information of bringing back true reconciliation of the truth that could heal the wounds of my people. I've found such a book in the pages of this vital document.

Dr. Jay Swallow
Co-founder, Two Rivers Native American Training Center
Bixby, Oklahoma

OVER THE YEARS, I HAVE BEEN HONORED and privileged to minister and just be with Alice Patterson. She is a person of integrity with a pure heart. I wish I could get this book into the hands of every pastor, politician, and leader in the nation. As I have observed the horrendous political divide in our nation and experienced the pain of it in my sphere of authority, I have cried out for the information in this book to be made known and available. As you read this, allow God to take you into His heart and His hope for our country. Just as our Father's perfect love casts out and does away with fear, so allow this book to change your heart and see how the church must move in this hour.

Rev. Merrie Cardin
Founder and Leader, Brazos Strategic Network

ALICE'S CANDID YET CHEWABLE ASSESSMENT of America's Christianity intermingled with racial politics makes a tough subject matter digestible. This gentle, courageous woman's spiritual insight and revelation will inform and tearfully enlighten you. If you seek truth, this truth will make you free!

Rev. Karen Hunter Harris
Medicine for the Heart Ministries, Inc.
Lakehills, Texas

ANDREW MURRAY STATES IN HIS BOOK *Covenants and Blessings*, "What a man believes moves and rules his whole being. It enters into him and becomes part of his very life." Alice portions out to us the process of her belief system—a journey of uncovering and discovering. This adventure in partnership with her husband and friends has unearthed profound spiritual truth about our nation and its lifelong political crisis. The contents of this writing will cause you to examine and re-cultivate your own "root value structure"—that which anchors your entire life. Alice is a "friend" to our nation; she is able to expose the "unspoken" and still offer a "cup of cool water," that becomes the spiritual salve for healing our nation. You be a friend to our nation too by acting on this book and placing it in the hands of your neighbors.

Hollis Kirkpatrick
Co-Founder, Servants to the City
Fort Worth, Texas

NEVER IN MY LIFE HAVE I KNOWN A WHITE PERSON with such a passion for Brown people, the American Hispanics. Alice Patterson demonstrates this in her hard-hitting book, Bridging the Racial & Political Divide. In it she reveals that she is not a mere theoretician, but one who proves her love in action. What is most amazing is the compatible, non-offensive manner in which she relates to the Hispanic community—including Sephardic Jews of Latino descent.

Dell F. Sanchez, PhD
Author, *The Last Exodus* and *Out from Hiding—Evidences of Sephardic Jewish Roots among Latinos*

BRIDGING THE RACIAL & POLITICAL DIVIDE is an essential part of the process for creating one nation under God. For over 20 years, I have known Alice to be a person whom God has called into the ministry of reconciliation. God has inspired her to address the essential underlying problems within the body of Christ that prevent us from truly being spiritual brothers and sisters. Unafraid of the criticism and unhindered by the threat of ostracism, she has accepted the challenge to be consistent in speaking the truth on issues most ministries have ignored or run away from to avoid controversy. As many of those wounded by the legacy of racial hatred have been crying out from the pain, an ear, a heart, and a voice have come to the front and now speaks clearly. Through the effective use of the spiritual gift of discernment and a strong prayer ministry, Alice has accurately identified the strongholds that plague us and presents the methods for bringing them down!

Dr. M. L. Johnson,
Author, *Overcoming Racism Through the Gospel*

IN 2003, GOD SUPERNATURALLY LED ME to Alice Patterson. I can remember the very moment God knitted my heart to hers. It was the day a friend forwarded an email to me written by Alice about citywide prayer and reconciliation. I read it immediately and I felt like I had found my counterpart. I had no idea who this woman was, but I knew she was going to be a part of my destiny. It was the beginning of this same year that God instructed me to launch a global prayer network, Jabez Prayer Network, which was going to be a racial-reconciliation endeavor. I wrote Alice immediately and not long after this, I received a call from her. This call was the start of a journey of a wonderful work of racial reconciliation in my life, as an African-American, with such an incredible and passionate governmental reconciler, Alice Patterson. Alice is my friend, but greater than this, she is God's voice echoing through the corridors of time crying out for America's wounds to be healed in the church and in the political realm. I endorse this woman of God and her heart for change.

Dr. Shirley K. Clark
Founder & Executive Director, Jabez Prayer Network, Plano, Texas

THE ONE WORD I WILL USE TO DESCRIBE THIS WORK is *passionate*. Alice is not just presenting an issue that she has studied. It is at the heart of who she is. She has experienced this. She has engaged herself in the midst of it. She is passionate about it. *Bridging the Racial & Political Divide* is a word that flows from her intimacy with the Lord and her relationship with Black America. It is a "now" word that will bring freedom to a people "still" enslaved. It is time for all of us to walk in complete freedom.

Dr. Thomas Schlueter
Author, *Keeper of the Keys* and *Return of the Priests*
Pastor, Prince of Peace Church, Arlington, Texas

IN THIS BOOK, MY GOOD FRIEND, ALICE PATTERSON, the granddaughter of a deceased Ku Klux Klan member, presents a thorough, incisive, serious, and compelling story about how God dealt with her concerning racism. Alice tells the heartfelt story of the principles she learned, the evil structures she discovered, and reveals the God-given strategies to dismantle the structures. This book touches on race relations, politics, hidden Black history, and most of all, repentance and reconciliation. A wealth of information can be learned from this rich and interesting study.

Willie F. Wooten
Author, *Breaking the Curse Off Black America*

ALICE PATTERSON IS A BRAVE WOMAN. She lives and ministers for God in the government arena, and she has learned well how to influence the political machine for righteousness. In this book she has taken the bold and courageous step of exposing pernicious racism in our nation and in our churches. This is a penetrating, provoking, and practical book that all who have a hope for reforming our society in our times must read and absorb!

C. Peter Wagner, Chancellor
Wagner Leadership Institute

DEDICATION

The book is dedicated to
Dr. C. L. Jackson, Pastor
Pleasant Grove Missionary Baptist Church
Houston, Texas.
Your leadership transcends generations,
cultural barriers, and political parties.
Thank you for your love for God's Word,
and for your courage to stand for truth
wherever you find it.

CONTENTS

Why are Black and White evangelicals who agree theologically so divided by race, especially in politics? This book is an invitation to step into the Grand Canyon of all divisions—the gulf between Black evangelicals who are Democrats and White evangelicals who are Republicans.

PART I – THE JOURNEY

I met José Gonzalez after I asked the Lord to show me how to reach Hispanics—who are pro-life, hard working, and pro-traditional marriage. He introduced me to corporate pain, the realization that an entire ethnic group can be wounded and pass their pain down to future generations. That encounter led to meetings with Hispanic leaders with no agenda but to listen. The presence of God, racial reconciliation, and divine connections of the heart were the result.

In 1995 I repented before African American Bishop Joseph Garlington on behalf of my grandfather and the Christian Right. I didn't repent for the values of conservatives, but for our insensitivity on the race issue. The sometimes-angry face of Christians on television is not the face of Jesus. Genuine repentance and humility disarms powers of darkness and are powerful when prayed by people who understand spiritual authority.

Chapter 3: Claiming Territory _____59

We demonstrated the power of prayer, blessing, and claiming territory for the Lord at the geographical center of Texas, the entrances into Odessa, Texas, and at an abortionist's office. The results were miraculous. When we are obedient to bless people, the Lord causes the blessing to remain—if the person we're blessing is a man of peace. If we bless someone who is not worthy of the blessing, our blessing releases God's righteousness to change the situation for his Kingdom.

Chapter 4: The Presence of God in the Political Arena_____69

The dragging death behind a pickup truck of African American James Byrd, Jr. in Jasper County, Texas, precipitated corporate repentance at a political convention for the sin of racism in the White church. That led to an opportunity to repent before Mr. Byrd's daughter for the murder of her father. A person in authority in the political arena or in a business can welcome the presence of God and move under Kingdom principles to transform their sphere of influence.

Chapter 5: Healing Hearts – Changing Lives _____83

Experiencing the presence of God in the public arena heals hearts and changes lives. Government officials and individuals must realize that they can give the Lord access into their sphere of government because God's power is released when government aligns with God's Kingdom.

Chapter 6: Hidden Black History_____99

At a meeting in a large church in Houston, David Barton of WallBuilders shared the long-suppressed truth about the history of Black Americans and the political process. The components are revealed for transformation from wounding to healing, and from deception to the truth of history.

Chapter 7: Systemic Racism _____117

While at a meeting in Washington, D. C., Dr. C. L. Jackson shared some shocking information that filled in the blanks about the racial and political divide among Black and White evangelicals. That piece of insight gave the perspective needed to understand the political breach and the grace to begin to do something about it.

Chapter 8: Influence vs. Power_____129

There is a difference between influence and power. It's the difference between being invited to dinners, receptions, and photo opportunities with elected officials and the real power of taking a seat at the decision-making table. Voting a straight party ticket is not the same as having power by being on the inside of the political party process. Information about how the system works has been withheld, but no longer.

PART II – THE REVELATION

Chapter 9: Evil Structures Exposed _____145

Dr. Chuck Pierce said, "Let the Lord show you Saul Structures in your life and ministry and how to dismantle them." As Chuck described Saul Structures, my thoughts raced to politics. *Oh my God, Chuck is describing a political party!* This was the first time I'd ever considered that an evil structure could be connected to and empowered by a political party. Upon further research and prayer, the Lord showed me the spiritual structures embedded in our two main political parties.

Chapter 10: The Jezebel Structure _____159

The Jezebel structure began by devaluing the lives of slaves, which is an ideology that devalues human life as a whole. A false theology believed by the Ku Klux Klan and others is called *British Israel*. This replacement theology teaches that White Christians replace the Jews to become the true Israel, and also advocates against interracial marriage. The White supremacist theology is the basis for Planned Parenthood's outreach to Black and Hispanic communities. Planned Parenthood was formed as a eugenics organization, which believed in a white superior race and focuses its activities in inner city neighborhoods populated by Black and Hispanic Americans. The founder worked to deceive Black pastors and the Black population to accept sterilization and eventually abortion, resulting in the genocide of over 17 million Black babies since 1973.

Chapter 11: False Worship for Economic Increase _____169

Dr. Jay Swallow teaches four things defile the land: false worship, broken covenants, sexual perversion, and the shedding of innocent blood. In our Western culture, we can readily see the defilement in sexual perversion, broken covenants, and the shedding of innocent blood. But it's not easy for us to recognize the worship of false gods. Our money declares *In God We Trust*. But how many political decisions are made because of economic considerations? Christians choose candidates and political parties because of promises that will put more money in *my* pocket (health care, social security, higher minimum wage, higher taxes on the rich). Dr. C. L. Jackson said, "We've substituted God for government. If we'll trust the Lord, He'll give us more than forty acres and a mule."

Chapter 12: The Ahab Structure _____185

The tragic consequences of misplaced trust are evident. However, in speaking to the Church at Thyatira, the Lord holds the Church responsible. He didn't reprimand Jezebel for her deception and seduction. That's her nature. He holds the one who tolerates Jezebel responsible. Queen Jezebel couldn't have exerted governmental authority without the cooperation or acquiescence of King Ahab, and God holds Ahab responsible. Ahab is a study in contradictions. He is a strong military leader yet weak spiritually. He surrenders and yields to intimidation. Ahab's big sin was passivity. Sometimes we pin things on spiritual apathy, but the correct word is *passivity*. There's a difference. Whereas *apathy* is a lack of interest, *passivity* is a lack of action.

Chapter 13: Tolerance—Virtue or Sin?

Tolerance is a virtue that most Americans value. However, the sin of tolerating Jezebel is why the Lord reprimanded the Church at Thyatira in Revelation 2. The Ahab structure through acquiescence and spiritual passivity empowers abortion, same-sex marriage, and big government as the solution to poverty. Deception is the hardest thing to recognize in yourself because being deceived is thinking you're right when you're wrong. Sometimes it's easier to be loyal to the teachings of legalism and deception than it is to act on the truth.

Chapter 14: Dismantling Unholy Structures

There are three areas where unholy structures must be dismantled: on a personal level, on a strategic spiritual level, and on a national governmental area. Dismantling unholy structures on a personal level and strategic spiritual level begins by aligning yourself with the truth and asking God to give you grace to accept it. We must repent for having believed a lie and prioritize personal intimacy with God. Wailing for the sins of our nation and for allowing ungodly structures to stand leads to revival, breakthrough, and transformation.

Chapter 15: Repairing the Altar of Worship

Worship is a powerful, strategic spiritual step to dismantle evil structures. We must praise, worship, and stand in the glory. When we reach a deep place of worship, that's where the Lord Himself wars. We must rise up in the spirit of Elijah to dismantle structures in both political parties. It's God who reigns, not a political party. America is waiting for godly believers of all ethnicities to engage in the political process.

FOREWORD
By Ed Silvoso

THIS BOOK BY ALICE PATTERSON is both groundbreaking and—let me warn you—controversial! It is groundbreaking because it invites you to go where few have gone, and to do what even fewer have done. It is controversial because she dares challenge traditional mindsets with biblical insights, first-hand experiences, and historical perspectives about the most divisive, explosive, disruptive, and still untamed dimension of society as far as the involvement of biblical Christians is concerned: politics. This book is indeed revolutionary!

At the very outset, Alice poses a sobering question: *Why are Black and White evangelicals, who agree theologically, so divided by race, especially in politics?* This book is devoted to providing the answer, not only to the causes of the divide but, most importantly, to show how to bridge it so that God's presence and power can be brought into the political arena to make this world a better place.

Alice's credentials to write on race reconciliation and politics are impeccable. As the granddaughter of a former Ku Klux Klan member, Alice's heart has been broken over both overt and unconscious racism, and she has since devoted her life to building bridges between ethnic groups. Though involved in a political party, she is first and foremost a follower of Jesus, and as such she is able to see beyond political parties and operate within a biblical grid that transcends parties to introduce us to God's way rather than man's.

It is time to learn how to bring God's goodness, mercy, wisdom, righteousness and power to the political arena. When I wrote *Anointed for Business* and its follow-up *Transformation*, I challenged readers to believe that God redeemed more than souls because He also redeemed the marketplace—business, education and government. Since then we have seen encouraging transformation in the business and education spheres, but not so much in the realm of government. The reason is that we have lacked a tool like the one Alice makes available here to approach the political arena with a grassroots healing message. The healing of our political process will produce a healthy domino effect because politics is the path to government, and government is the catalytic component in the marketplace since it regulates the other two—business and education.

In my upcoming book, *Anointed for Politics—How to Swim in Dirty Water Without Drinking It*, I make the point that the ongoing war between political parties in America is not God's battle. He is not for one and against the other. God's purposes are not found in the forces that make them different, but in the potential synergy of those differences to get the job done. This is necessary because as a result of sin we live in societies filled with antagonistic pairings such as rich and poor, management and labor, Blacks and Whites, men and women, and on the American political stage, Republicans and Democrats. These antagonistic pairs are opposing pyramids that came into being when the cube they were originally part of was dissected and separated by sin, and the ensuing power structures began to serve themselves by attacking and assaulting each other instead of synergizing for the greater common good.

How long have we wished for the cube to be rejoined? We have hope. Is it not interesting that Paul's description of the manifestation of the love of God in the world (Ephesians 3:18) is presented as a cube, as are the dimensions of the New Jerusalem where nations will dwell (Revelation 21:16)? Indeed, Christ came to bring wholeness to all things, and the process must begin now. For this to happen, enlightened Christians need to model the healing message that Alice Patterson so eloquently presents here for God's will to be done on earth, and especially in the political arena.

This book will challenge and convict you, and in the end it will also inspire and empower you. Be ready for a life-changing experience!

Ed Silvoso
Author, *Anointed for Business* **and** *Transformation*
www.transformourworld.org

Introduction

*"Our lives begin to end the day we
become silent about things that matter."*
—Dr. Martin Luther King, Jr.

WHY ARE BLACK AND WHITE EVANGELICALS, who agree theologically, so divided by race—especially in politics? Somebody hand me a can opener so I can open this can of worms! Of course, it would be easier to just put that can of smelly stuff back on the shelf. Some would say, "Now is not the time. America is divided by race."

The election of President Barack Obama simply exposed the divisions. In our nation, things are a little touchy right now. I could play it safe. That would ensure that some very important relationships—both Black and White—would remain intact.

I'm known as a reconciler—a person who bridges denominations and races. Why jeopardize my reputation?

Who am I to tackle race in America? Especially race in politics! I'm White. My grandfather was a Ku Klux Klan member. I'm probably the last person most would choose. Then again, maybe God broke my heart over racism for this very purpose.

I've spent the last 16 years focused on race. Papa, as we called my dad's father, never talked to me about his Klan activities. Race, discrimination, and bigotry aren't topics of conversation in most White families. Papa passed away over two decades before I started asking questions about race, wondering what he really did when he hid his shame under the white hood of a Klansman. Although there were no family sources I could go to, I've been on a quest to understand. I've read books and watched documentaries. I've broached the subject with a few Black friends who would let me gaze through the window of their pain.

This is my story about how God dealt with me about racism, the principles I learned, the evil structures I discovered, and some strategies the Lord revealed to dismantle the structures. My journey began when I was Field Director of Texas Christian Coalition (TXCC). *That's an unlikely place for concern about race*, you might possibly say, and you'd be right. Christian Coalition, which no longer exists, was predominantly a Caucasian organization. I was a grassroots organizer in what the media calls the *Christian Right*. If you're a Person of Color, that probably doesn't elicit warm, fuzzy feelings. In fact, you may be tempted to close this book right now.

I am asking you, "Please be brave. Stay with me through a journey of discovery." I believe a case is to be made that will illustrate some principles. At the same time, the journey is important to demonstrate the magnitude of the issue.

Do I need to remind anyone about our Pledge of Allegiance? Growing up in America, all of us recited these famous words:

> I pledge allegiance to the flag of the United States of America and to the republic for which it stands: one nation under God, indivisible, with liberty and justice for all.

Were we giving *lip service*? Or are we willing to practice those powerful words of freedom? Our nation is a symbol of freedom to other nations. Now more than ever is time to put our words into action.

When Black, White, and Hispanic Christians come together in multi-denominational settings to focus on transforming cities, we can bring up race, pray together, forgive each other, and quickly agree to work toward our broader vision of transforming nations. However, the atmosphere changes when we add politics to the mix—especially Democrat vs. Republican. Things get tense. No matter your ethnicity or political party, you may become defensive or suspicious. This is a time to check your heart. It may be beating a little faster at this moment. Why? We're standing on the brink of the Grand Canyon of all divisions. It is the deepest and widest breach. It's the gap between Black Christians who are mostly Democrats and White Christians who are mostly Republicans.

> The Lord is looking for someone to build up the wall and stand in the gap before Him for the land.

The Lord says He is looking for someone to build up the wall and stand in the gap before Him for the land. He's still searching for that person.

> "I searched for a man among them who would build up the wall and stand in the gap before Me for the land, so that I would not destroy it; but I found no one." (Ezekiel 22:30)

Are you willing to step into this gap—this wide, expansive racial and political divide? Are you willing to stand there—not just rush through? Are you willing to be the one who satisfies the Lord's long-ing to find someone that He can use to heal our land? Saying *yes* re-quires that you climb down into this gully. Into this wide political and racial divide. Into this broken place. You will be required to stand in this place of brokenness long enough to deal with tough issues so the Lord can heal His body and eventually our nation. It sounds easy, but it must be challenging or the Lord wouldn't need to search for such a person. He could just choose from the millions waiting in line for the assignment. "Choose me, Lord. Over here! I'll be the one!"

Sadly, a long line of people isn't waiting to stand in this gap. Who wants to deal with grief, pain and least of all *emotions*? No, the Lord is still on a quest to find someone who will give Him access to wounded places by standing in the gap. He wants to restore some bruised and broken lives. And He wants to heal the land we call America in the process. Will the search stop with you? Take my hand and let's walk down into this breach together. Come with me on a journey.

My job as Field Director of TXCC was to organize county chapters to mobilize pro-life, pro-family voters. I'd been involved in politics in various organizations and campaigns since 1984. I resigned my posi-tion with Texas Christian Coalition in 1996 to pursue racial healing and social transformation. In 1994 the Lord moved race to the front burner in my life. You'll read how that happened in the following pages. For now, I pray that the things I say and the way I say them will not cause further pain, no matter your ethnicity or political persuasion.

This book is not merely one person's journey. It's a manual that will equip and prepare you to use spiritual tools to bring healing to individuals and to nations. The context is politics, or some would say that it is the *government mountain*. It's about social transformation in government. It's about the political arena.

In the last prayer that Jesus prayed for His disciples and for those who would follow them, He gives us a key for how social transformation will begin.

> "That they may all be one, even as Thou, Father, art
> in Me, and I in Thee, that they also may be in Us;
> that the world may believe that Thou didst send
> Me....that they may be one just as We are one...that
> they may be perfected in unity, that the world may
> know that Thou didst send Me, and didst love them,
> even as Thou didst love Me." (John 17:21-23)

If we read that passage literally, it gives the key to evangelizing nations. The world will realize that Jesus is God when we, His followers, are one. When the world knows that the Lord is the One True God and that He sent Jesus to pay the penalty for every man's sin, millions will be saved. When we are one, the world will know Who Jesus really is and that He loves, forgives, restores, and transforms.

> The world will realize that Jesus is God when we, His followers, are one.

Fine. That sounds easy. Let's just be one. If it were easy, it already would have happened. Even the twelve disciples who lived with Jesus for three years were not one. They argued over who would be greatest. James and John went so far as to get their mother into the squabble.

It stands to reason then that if our functioning as one is the first step to city and national transformation, Satan will do whatever he can to prevent it. That explains why Satan has a structure—a network of evil—that resists healing and reconciliation. I had never given any thought to a *structure* in a political context until August 2004 when several leaders of the United States Strategic Prayer Network (USSPN) were in Louisiana for a meeting convened by Louisiana coordinators, Roger and Charlotte Merschbrock. I was there as the Texas Coordinator along with leaders from Oklahoma, Mississippi, and Florida. Dr. Chuck Pierce, who was leader of the network, spoke in Baton Rouge about *Saul Structures*. His admonition was to *let God show you the Saul Structures in your life and ministry and how to dismantle them.* Then Chuck began to enlighten us on these unholy structures.

Oh, my God, my thoughts were racing. *Chuck is describing a political party!* I was stunned. Although I had a political background, I had never associated a political party with a demonic structure. Chuck's words resonated in my spirit and those thoughts dominated my thinking for the next several months and now years. I searched the Word of God, prayed and questioned spiritual leaders who might have insight. I could not put down the concept of *Saul Structures* then, and I still can't. In fact, that revelation is the reason for writing this book. I'm driven by it. This structure in America most adversely affects Black and Hispanic Americans. I am compelled to disclose it whether I'm received or not. You probably want to understand more about this structure, but stay with me through the journey the Lord has been leading me on. The journey is as important as the revelation about structures and how to dismantle them. The truth revealed is shocking—to say the least!

The unholy structures are positioned for maximum effectiveness in government—in the political arena. I will expose what empowers

them and what we can do to overcome them. The structures have succeeded over many generations in America. They are keeping the Body
of Christ divided, and millions of people, especially many Black
Americans, chained in poverty and hopelessness.

God is concerned about politics. Don't let the devil tell you otherwise. He has manifested His presence in political situations. In fact, I
can say without hesitation that I have
experienced the presence of God more
profoundly in governmental settings
than in church or religious events. I've
seen lives transformed before my eyes
as God moved in supernatural ways
in a political context. Although God

> God is concerned about politics. Don't let the devil tell you otherwise.

has moved powerfully in the governmental sphere, we have not been
successful in dismantling the demonic network of principalities controlling this area. That's what we will explore in this book.

So where were we? Oh, yes. I was about to open a can of worms.
It's worse than a can of worms. It's a place of open wounds, generational mistrust and suspicion. You're still with me? May I borrow a can
opener? Hold your nose and hang on to your heart.

TERMINOLOGY

AS I THINK ABOUT WHO IS READING THIS BOOK, my heart is to give honor. When we come to the *race question*, emotions bombard our thoughts. What word do I use to describe a *Person of Color*? I know that I'm stepping into territory where emotions run deep. It depends on the part of the country where you live as to the proper terminology to use. Our American history is full of painful memories for many Americans. The last thing I want to do is add to the pain. The dilemma is real when it comes to how to approach the subject without adding to discrimination and dishonor.

Several years ago I was in a meeting of Texans who are of Mexican descent. We were having an open discussion free from discrimination. A businessman from West Texas said, "Who am I? Am I Hispanic, Latino, Mexican, Tejano, Mexicano, Chicano?" Others in the room understood the quandary regarding self-identity.

In this book I will use *Hispanic*.

Individuals from different parts of the country call themselves different things regarding their race. I remember a political meeting over 15 years ago when a Houston woman exclaimed, "I am not a hyphenated American. I'm an American!" She was reacting to the term *African*

29

American. If you're from the Northeast, Northwest and some other regions of our nation, that is probably your terminology of choice.

I've spent the last several years listening and trying to understand the perception of *People of Color* regarding race. Even the question of capitalization can bring dishonor. Grammar experts say to capitalize formal names of races and ethnic groups such as African American or Asian, but not to capitalize skin colors, such as the *black community* or *white residents.* However, in this book, I'm breaking the rules because I want to give honor—even in grammar. Therefore, I'm capitalizing every mention of race—Black, White, Hispanic, etc.,—whether it's a noun or an adjective.

I've paid attention to Black pastor friends in the South, where I'm from. They seem to favor the terms *Blacks* or *Black Americans.* However, even in the South, some denominations prefer *African American.* Given my culture and the terminology that my Black friends prefer, I will use the term *Black* most of the time. When talking about my childhood and describing the one-room *Colored school,* I will use italics, meaning that's not my choice of words but the terminology of the day. I pray that my description using the term it was called in 1952 will not be seen as a pejorative term.

As you can see, it's not easy to write about race—or, for that matter, to read about race. However, we can get through this together. It's my prayer that we will all be better for the journey.

PART I

THE JOURNEY

Chapter 1

✦

RACIAL HEALING
IN THE POLITICAL ARENA

I DON'T REMEMBER HOW I FOUND OUT. I just grew up knowing it. Papa, Dad's father, had once joined the Ku Klux Klan (KKK) in the early 1900s in Oklahoma. The family moved to Texas in 1924 when my father was six years old, and Papa's Klan activity ceased. I thought the KKK was something like a volunteer sheriff's posse—a citizen group that helped to enforce the law. That's a genuine case of *whitewash*, but it's really what I thought. I didn't ask questions. I can't explain how I could live my teenage years during the Civil Rights Movement in the 1960s without being affected by it, but I did. Now I'm saddened by the thought. But at that time I was ignorant and in my *little White world* in Earth, Texas, *population 1,087 with less than 30 Black folk.*

I remember the time I went inside the *Colored school* on the grounds of rural Springlake-Earth Independent School District in the Panhandle of Texas to deliver a note to the teachers. The *Colored school* was a small white stucco building among four large brick modern structures for White students. There were less than fifteen students—most of them were elementary school age. I knew that Black kids were in the separate, inferior school, but I didn't ask why. I didn't question the way things were. I didn't watch the news on television or read national newspapers. I know it sounds impossible, but I lived through my high school years without realizing that there was a struggle going on among Black folk for basic human rights. In 1970 after I was married, I remember seeing a Black guy in a red bandana with his fist in the air during the singing of the Star Spangled Banner at a college football game in Portales, New Mexico. I was shocked, but I was not compelled to find out why he was angry at our nation.

The Race Question

The race question didn't surface in my life until 1991. As Field Director of Texas Christian Coalition (TXCC),[1] I traveled to the Rio Grande Valley, the southernmost part of Texas on the border between the United States and Mexico. The Rio Grande Valley is 80 to 95 percent Hispanic. However, Hispanics, who are pro-life and family-oriented, were absent from Christian Coalition, a mostly White organization. I prayed, *Lord, how do I reach Hispanics?*

Three years later at the Harvey Hotel in Dallas, three girlfriends who were Christian Coalition chapter leaders and I attended a Strategic Christian Services seminar hosted by Dennis Peacocke. There we met a man I could ask about connecting with Hispanics. José Gonzalez, a leader in one of the government breakout sessions, taught political science and mentored future Latin American political leaders at Regent University in Virginia Beach.

"José, how do I reach Hispanics?" José began to talk about the Alamo—the mission in San Antonio where Texans fought the battle for independence against the advancing Mexican army in 1836. I'm thinking, *I didn't ask for a history lesson. I want to know how to reach Hispanics.*

Corporate Pain

José introduced our group to *corporate pain*—the concept that an entire ethnic group can be wounded. Not only is it possible for whole people groups to be wounded, but they can and do pass their pain down from one generation to another. José's point wasn't whether the battle of the Alamo was either good or bad. His point was this: Mexican citizens and Texans may view the same historical event through different colored *glasses*. One sees it as a victory and reason to celebrate. The other sees it as a source of broken covenant, pain, anger, and theft of their property. By the way, this is not a Hispanic issue only. There were Hispanics called *Tejanos* fighting for independence inside the Alamo. And Hispanics—the Mexican army—were fighting for Mexican sovereignty outside the Alamo. So modern-day Hispanics can either celebrate or grieve. It's all about perspective—which *glasses* you wear to view a historical event.

> It's all about perspective—which *glasses* you wear to view a historical event.

As José expounded on the Alamo, instantly my grandfather's Klan involvement came to mind. Conviction slammed into my spirit, and I knew I had to repent. The weight of Papa's sin, as well as my own insensitivity to the pain of others—particularly Black and Hispanic Americans, sat like a concrete block on my chest. I telephoned my boss and Chairman of TXCC to share with him the incredible revelation José shared. *Together we must repent for the sin of racism. It was urgent. We had to ask the Lord to forgive our own sins, as well as the sins of my grandfather and other White Christians.* My boss lived in the Dallas area so he drove over to the hotel. Then the five leaders of the TXCC along with José huddled together in the hotel lobby as we repented individually and corporately for our sins. We repented for not understanding and for not trying to understand. We asked forgiveness for our insensitivity—for living lives untouched by the pain of others. I repented for Papa and for millions of White Americans like him who see themselves as superior.

I can't begin to describe the emotions flooding my mind and heart as we knelt together in the presence of the Lord. This was the culmination of a four-year prayer to understand how to reach Hispanics. But it was much more. It was the beginning of my journey into the area of race in America. It was the crushing truth that my grandfather had a part in the generational pain still troubling Black Americans and other *People of Color* in our nation. It began my journey into the racial divide in this nation. At the beginning, it was just with Hispanics, but later my focus became Black Americans. I had misjudged Blacks, as you will see later in this book. But the gate into ethnic America had been unlocked. God was opening my eyes and my heart to America's wounds, and I would never be the same.

Before we left Dallas, I asked José, "Now what do I do?"

"Hold a meeting with Hispanic leaders with no agenda but to listen."

"Will you come to the meeting?"

"No, you don't need me."

That terrified me. First, you never convene a meeting in the political arena without an agenda. Second, I knew very few Hispanics. Third, I didn't have a clue what I was doing. But José encouraged me to continue to listen to the voice of the Lord. I determined to obey Him. That was October 1994.

I asked friends for names of Hispanics we could invite to the meeting. The Marriott River Center was secured in San Antonio for the first meeting in mid-January of 1995. A Costa Rican businessman agreed to fund an overnight stay and meals for our Hispanic guests.

A Divine Encounter

On January 2, 1995, something happened that I will never forget. You may have had a similar experience, where the Lord breaks through your consciousness and puts down a spiritual marker that you can go back to over and over. That's what happened to me. I was sitting on my couch having my quiet time. My Bible fell open to Isaiah 58, the *fasting chapter*, which I always try to dodge because I don't like to fast. It was two weeks before the scheduled meeting with Hispanic leaders. Since race was on my mind, I read Isaiah 58 with my *race glasses* on.

It said, "Cry loudly, do not hold back; raise your voice like a trumpet and declare to My people their transgression" (Isaiah 58:1). Isaiah goes on to tell how God's people loved to be in God's presence, to seek Him and to keep His law. They were fervent in their religiosity—even fasting—and upset that the Lord wasn't noticing their sacrifice. Then the Lord says, "Is not this the fast which I have chosen, to loosen the bonds of wickedness, to undo the bands of the yoke and to let the oppressed go free, and to break every yoke?" (verse 6).

My heart swelled as I realized the Lord Himself was speaking to me about the sin of racism. "Those from among you will rebuild the ancient ruins; you will raise up the age-old foundations; and you will be called the repairer of the breach, the restorer of the streets in which to dwell" (verse 12).

I called José. "I have to tell you what happened this morning." I read the scriptures to him. When I finished reading verse 12, he sighed, "Hallelujah. Do you know what a breach is?"

"No."

"It's a wound, a spiritual rupture. It could be caused by something that happened years ago—even generations ago—and it's been allowed to fester because it's never been dealt with by the Spirit. It may look normal on the outside, but when someone bumps it, it breaks open and the unhealed wound is revealed."

Reconciliation Begins

After that conversation, José agreed to come to San Antonio for our first meeting. Twenty-five Hispanic leaders from across Texas showed up. Since we didn't have an agenda, I didn't know what to do. José counseled, "Just share your heart."

So I turned to Isaiah 58 and read verses one through twelve. I shared about growing up in Earth, Texas, a small town where Mexican migrant farm workers came through to harvest crops. I shared about trying to remember Hispanic kids in my class. It was like they were invisible. Later I understood their quietness as possible insecurity. Plus they were most likely uncomfortable speaking English. In fact, a Catholic priest later shared, "When I was in the fifth grade, I was sent to the principal's

> "I was sent to the principal's office and spanked for speaking Spanish. They didn't realize that they were punishing me for my identity— for who I am."

office and spanked for speaking Spanish. They didn't realize that they were punishing me for my identity—for who I am."

I prayed a prayer of repentance. I repented as the granddaughter of a Ku Klux Klan member. I detailed the sins of racism, pride, superiority, and insensitivity. José recently reminded me that I wept with black mascara running down my face and cried, "Lord, please forgive us for regarding Hispanics only as the people who mow our lawns." As I prayed, an astounding thing happened. The tangible presence of God gently settled on everyone in the room! That was the first, but certainly not the last, time that I experienced the Lord's manifest presence in meetings convened in the political arena. In fact, I have experienced the pronounced presence of God more in political and governmental settings than I've ever experienced in strictly religious settings. The Lord wants to invade and transform every sphere of society—the family, religion, business, education, media, arts and entertainment, as well as government. The Lord places His anointing on those attempting to bring unity across racial, denominational, and political barriers, because it is an answer to His last prayer in John 17:21 that *we would be one.*

> PRINCIPLE: When we align ourselves with God's heart, He opens doors for us to reveal His heart to others. God's heart is for reconciliation.

Immediately after I shared Isaiah 58, Dr. Dell Sanchez of The Life Chapel in San Antonio, who is a former social worker and founded a broadcasting network, spoke up. "If you want to understand Hispanics, there are two things you must deal with—inferiority and ignorance. Not intellectual ignorance—far from it—but ignorance of how things work in the political arena. Will you show us how things work, and will you allow us to succeed in your society?"

"Yes! The answer is yes!"

> **PRINCIPLE**: God will use the sin and pain in our own lives and ancestry as an access point for healing and restoration in the lives of others.

God Opens Hearts

The Lord gave us eight hours in His presence dealing with matters of the heart. Feelings of inferiority. Hurt. Anger. Confusion. Suspicion. One of the men said, "I don't know where I fit. Am I Hispanic, Latino, Chicano, Mexican American? Who am I? I don't fit with Whites, and I don't fit with Blacks. Where is my place?"

During the break, Stephen Cervantes, a licensed marriage and family therapist and leader in the local chapter of Christian Coalition, came up to me. "I'm a trained counselor, Alice. If you'll let me, I think I can facilitate dialogue." Stephen skillfully asked probing questions. Matters of the heart were gently laid bare for all to see.

When I look back on those early meetings, I see what a supernatural thing it was for members of one culture, who admittedly feel inferior, to open their hearts to the *dominant culture*, as they call Whites. During those moments of honest discussion in God's presence, He bound us eternally to one another.

I've heard the argument, "I wasn't there. Neither I nor my family owned slaves. Why should I repent for something I didn't do?" My response is this, "If you see someone who is wounded by another's racism, even if it isn't your own, why wouldn't you want to repent if it means someone will be healed and set free?"

> **PRINCIPLE:** Humility and repentance open wounded hearts for healing to take place.

I can't emphasize the importance of simply acknowledging that racism exists. In 2006 I was invited by my friend, Pastor Dwight McKissic, to Cornerstone Baptist Church, an exciting, large, primarily Black congregation in Arlington, Texas, to receive the Phoebe Award for my work in the Black community. In accepting the award, I mentioned my grandfather's KKK membership and repented for racism. When I sat down, a handsome young adult knelt before me and draped himself over my shoulders. He said, "I've heard my father talk about what happened to him just because he's Black. I thought how can one person do that to another? Why can't a White person just admit that there is racism in America? Can't somebody just say they're sorry? I've prayed that prayer for a long time, and here you are answering my prayer." He kept thanking me and later called me to tell me how much he was impacted. It's hard for a White person to understand how important this is, but it's foundational in healing America's wounds.

The next meeting took place in March 1995—again in San Antonio—at the historic Menger Hotel across the street from the Alamo. Because he had masterfully led us at the prior meeting, I appointed Stephen as the emcee. About 75 people gathered, including a Hispanic State Representative and a Polish American Catholic priest! Surprise of surprises—a Black pastor was asked to lead the opening prayer! *I thought this was about Hispanics,* I mused. But the Lord had other plans. Greg Jackson, a tall, handsome, military officer and elder at New Life Christian Center, a mostly Black congregation, was there representing his pastor who had been asked to pray. I thought Greg and the Catholic priest would probably leave after their part on the program, but both stayed. I opened by sharing my heart, and the Lord came in the same, tangible way.

God Has His Own Agenda

During the course of the meeting with Stephen chairing, his Anglo wife Tonna raised her hand several different times, but Stephen didn't call on her. Finally, she stood to her feet and said, "Stephen! I've got something to say!" Then Tonna turned to Greg, the elder from New Life Christian Center, and said, "My grandfather was a Grand Wizard of the Ku Klux Klan. Will you forgive me and my ancestors for all we've done...?" Tonna could hardly get the words out of her mouth before Greg rushed across the room and wrapped his arms around her, speaking and demonstrating his forgiveness. I'll never forget the sight of Tonna's long blonde hair on the shoulder of Greg's tall, lean frame.

No one but the Lord could orchestrate that! In 1995, while we were experiencing reconciliation and the presence of God in the political arena, we had no idea that God was speaking the same thing to different people. Promise Keepers, an evangelical ministry dedicated to uniting men to become *godly influences,* filled stadiums with men worshipping and humbling themselves before each other in genuine reconciliation. Dr. C. Peter Wagner, President of Global Harvest Ministries and prolific author, coined the phrase *identificational repentance* meaning that individuals can repent by standing in the gap as a representative for the sins of their forefathers. He teaches that both Daniel and

Nehemiah identified with the sins of their fathers and repented for them.

Daniel prayed, "Open shame belongs to us, O lord, to our kings, our princes, and our fathers, because we have sinned against Thee" (Daniel 9:8). "O Lord, in accordance with all Your righteous acts, let now Your anger and Your wrath turn away from Your city Jerusalem, Your holy mountain; for because of *our sins and the iniquities of our fathers*, Jerusalem and Your people have become a reproach to all those around us" (Daniel 9:16, emphasis added). Nehemiah confessed the "sins of the sons of Israel which we have sinned against You. I and my father's house have sinned. We have acted very corruptly against You..." (Nehemiah 1:6).

Stepping into a Movement

The meeting in San Antonio with Hispanics took place in the political arena, not the prayer movement. Without realizing it or being directly connected, we had stepped into a worldwide movement based on prayer, reconciliation, and revival. We simply heard the Lord and obeyed. He led us every step of the way.

Later in that meeting, Susan Weddington, my closest friend and also White, stood up in the back and repented for racism. Later Susan said to me, "Something strange is going on. Blacks and Hispanics have started talking to me in elevators and other places. That's never happened to me before."

"You're different, Susan. The racism in your life is gone and it shows on your face. You're approachable now." Almost a year earlier, Susan had been elected Vice Chairman of the Republican Party of Texas. God had prepared her heart in this meeting for the way He would use her publicly in racial reconciliation when she would become chairman three years later.

Before you think this is a veiled attempt to make you a Republican, relax. This is not an invitation to join the Republican Party. If you're a Democrat, take your faith and values into your party and make a difference. God chose Susan because she was willing to give Him access; she was able to then use her influence because of her position as chairman. You'll see how that happened later. If you have been wounded by Republicans, let me pray for you right now.

> *Father, I ask You to forgive me on behalf of Republicans*
> *who have wounded, offended, disrespected, or disappointed*
> *my friend in any way. I repent for overt as well as uncon-*
> *scious racism. I ask you to heal every hurt, Lord. I humble*
> *myself before You and this reader. Thank You for the blood*
> *of Jesus that cleanses us and for Your Holy Spirit that re-*
> *stores us. I pray that memories and perceptions will not*
> *hinder this reader from finishing this book in Jesus' name.*

Prayer and Repentance at the Alamo

During the meeting at the Alamo, I really wanted us to take communion together, but this was a political meeting and I didn't know how to maneuver that. Dell Sanchez had brought some *pan dulce,* Mexican sweet bread. I asked everyone to get a piece of pan dulce and go in mixed ethnic groups of three or four across the street to the Alamo. "Take the pan dulce, break it, share it, and pray together as you share the *friendship bread.* Ask the Lord to forgive us for our division and for not loving and honoring each other. Ask the Lord to forgive the historical divisions signified by the shedding of blood on these grounds over 150 years ago." Today we would call what we did a *prophetic act*. Then it was just blind obedience.

Even after these profound meetings, in the beginning I wrote off the Black community as a target for my outreach. Although I viewed pro-life Hispanics as a potential voting block for conservative issues, I misjudged Black Americans. Because Black voters comprise the most loyal segment of the Democratic base, I equated Black values with the values of the Democratic Party. I didn't know that the majority of Black Americans are pro-life, although huge majorities support a political party that is not.

Many Christians, especially People of Color, who vote a straight Democratic ticket don't realize that there is a document called a *party platform*. Elected delegates to state and national Democratic and Republican conventions vote to approve their party's platform. "The platform declares to the public that party's vision, beliefs, values, legislative plan and policy positions on important issues of the day."[2] The Democratic Party platform supports tax-funded abortion through all nine months of pregnancy. It also places rights for sexual orientation on the same level as civil rights for minorities, among other things.[3]

In addition to the party platform difference, many Democratic senators consistently voted against strict constructionist Supreme Court nominees like Clarence Thomas, John Roberts, and Samuel Alito. Strict constructionists oppose rewriting the Constitution to (1) oppose school prayer, (2) protect abortion, (3) endorse same-sex marriage, and (4) prohibit religious symbols on public property. There was a time when I thought Black Americans were pro-abortion and anti-school prayer because the party they support holds those positions, but I was wrong. Terribly wrong. Both Gallup and Pew polls show that

White evangelicals (83%) and all Blacks (65%) are the two most stable groups in opposition to same-sex marriage in America. Black evangelicals would be even higher than White evangelicals if they had been polled according to religious preference. An ABC News/Beliefnet poll found that Blacks are more likely than Whites to oppose abortion. Blacks were also more likely to oppose embryonic stem-cell research. Polls have consistently found between 70 to 80 percent of Blacks favor school prayer. Blacks are more likely than Whites to support parental choice in education, including vouchers.[4] In fact, poll after poll indicates that Blacks are more conservative than Whites on every moral issue of our day. I misjudged Black Americans and their values. In addition to my wrong perceptions, I didn't understand the corporate mindset.

---

[1] Christian Coalition was a national organization founded in 1989 by Dr. Pat Robertson, founder of the Christian Broadcasting Network, and led by Ralph Reed, Jr., one of the most strategic political organizers in America. I got involved in it, not because I was a fan of Pat Robertson's, but because I knew the grassroots plan would work. Christian Coalition focused on three things: (1) building coalitions with other pro-life, pro-family organizations, (2) recruiting a person in each church, who under the authority of his pastor, would register voters, distribute nonpartisan voter guides and educate about public policy issues and (3) enlisting activists in each political precinct to identify voters and get them to the polls.

[2] Democrats & Republicans in Their Own Words, National Party Platforms on Specific Biblical Issues, 2. http://www.justiceatthegate.org.

[3] Justice at the Gate prepared party platform comparisons called *Democrats & Republicans In Their Own Words* on four Biblical issues of abortion, homosexuality, school prayer and school choice plus a special issue on civil rights. You may read and download the comparisons online or order them by calling (210) 677-8214. http://www.justiceatthegate.org.

[4] http://abcnews.go.com/sections/us/DailyNews/poll010702.

Chapter 2

CORPORATE PAIN

ONE OF THE GREATEST DIFFERENCES in People of Color and Whites is whether we think *corporately* or *individually*. Ed Silvoso,[1] founder of Harvest Evangelism and a mentor to me, teaches that Whites are the only ethnic group in America that does not have a corporate identity. If you're White, you most likely see life through *individual* glasses. You make decisions based on yourself, your family, your business, your church, and your personal self-interests. Even White evangelical theology is vertical Christianity. It's mostly about you—your personal relationship with the Lord, your personal growth, and your personal holiness.

If you're a Person of Color, you most likely see life through *corporate glasses*. Everyone in your people group is connected as family. You understand *community*. That explains the pain Black folk experienced while watching news reports of Black American Rodney King, who was beaten by four White police officers in Los Angeles in 1991. "The spark came in April 1992 when all four officers were cleared of assault. Within hours, violence erupted across the city's Black neighborhoods. Fifty-five people were killed in several days of rioting, looting and retaliatory attacks against Whites and Asians. About 2,000 people were injured, and another 1200 arrested."[2]

When Whites saw the Rodney King beating on television, they thought, *King had been drinking. He was resisting arrest. Yes, there was too much force. The police didn't need to kick and club the man.* But when they turned off the television, they could forget it. It didn't personally affect them. Not so with Black folk who viewed the news coverage. They saw the White establishment wrongfully beating a member of their own family. The beating plus the ruling of the jury to let the four officers go free touched a deep wound. Corporate outrage and corporate violence erupted.

If you're Black, you may think Whites could forget about it because Rodney King was Black. If it had been a White guy who was beaten by four Black police officers, Whites would have erupted. Not so. There is no connection between most White people outside their immediate family. The perception by Whites would have been the same. And nothing would have happened corporately.

America—Divided by Race

The year that the Lord expanded my education about race was a year America was divided by race. The year 1995 was the year when O. J. Simpson was tried for the murder of his wife and Ron Goldman. Whites thought he was guilty. Most Blacks thought he was innocent. Why? Because many Blacks have been pulled over by police and questioned simply because of racial profiling. They've witnessed the disparity in justice between Blacks and Whites. Even though a few Blacks thought that O. J. Simpson probably killed both of them, most rejoiced that a Black guy finally had enough money to access White man's justice.

It was an amazing year for the Lord to speak to me about racism in America. In addition to the O. J. Simpson trial, it was right after Louis Farrakhan's Million Man March in Washington, D.C. Race was front and center. That year I convened three meetings with Hispanics and introduced the subject of racism to our entire TXCC organization at our state banquet in San Antonio in November.

If it would have been appropriate to have an altar call at a TXCC banquet, the altars would have been filled. As I looked out at the audience of about 500 people, eyes were brimming with tears and hearts were wide open. At this statewide gathering in San Antonio, we were very much aware that a small contingency from the *political left* attended the meeting. Generally antagonistic to the *Religious Right*, the media also attended. However, the presence of God enveloped the place.

The Sunday morning edition of the *San Antonio Express-News* displayed prominently a color picture of our keynote speaker, Texas Supreme Court Justice Raul Gonzalez, holding a Bible near his face. The article could not have been more positive if I had written it myself. It was amazing!

PRINCIPLE: Genuine repentance and humility disarm powers of darkness. Humility and repentance are as powerful as aggressive spiritual warfare prayers prayed by people who understand spiritual authority.

Call to Prayer and Fasting

A couple of weeks later I received an invitation to the Bill Bright Fasting and Prayer Gathering in Los Angeles. I knew I was supposed to be there. José Gonzalez had put my name on the list. Cathe Halford, my friend and TXCC Training Director, went with me.

The Fasting and Prayer Gathering was impressive with the Who's Who in Christian America leading us in prayer. It was okay, but I knew it wasn't why we were in Los Angeles. As Cathe and I walked through the hallways on the last day, I noticed a flier advertising LA '95, a meeting in the same facility on a parallel track to the Bill Bright one. I recognized Cindy Jacobs,[3] author of *Possessing the Gates of the Enemy*, and John Dawson, author of *Taking Our Cities for God*, because I'd read both of their books. I mentioned to Cathe, "Let's see if we can get into this meeting cheap enough. If not, let's go back to the hotel room and ask God why we're here." The attendants at the LA '95 registration table let us in for $10 each. Then a supervisor came over and reprimanded them. The people behind us had to pay the full price. We *knew* we were in the right place.

The LA '95 meeting was incredible. Peter Wagner defined *identificational repentance*. Cindy Jacobs taught about the children of Israel experiencing famine in the land for three years. During that time, King David sought the presence of God. And the Lord showed him that it was because of what Saul had done to the Gibeonites. "It is for Saul and his bloody house, because he put the Gibeonites to death" (II Samuel 21:1). Then King David went to the Gibeonites and asked, "What should I do for you? And how can I make atonement that you may bless the inheritance of the Lord?" The king asked for seven of Saul's sons, who were hanged to set the record straight. Cindy confirmed to us that sometimes we must deal with the sins of the past to receive blessings in the present.

New Vocabulary for Reconciliation

The Lord was giving us vocabulary for what we had been doing for over a year. It was amazing. One of the most moving things happening at LA '95 was that people from Los Angeles were called to come to the stage. There was a Korean couple whose store had been destroyed during the Rodney King riots. At one point, Black California prayer leader, Charles Doolittle, who was also a police officer, got on his knees and started to repent in detail on behalf of Blacks whose pain and anger fueled the violence. He also repented on behalf of the police department. Charles, tall and slender, was even tall on his knees as compared to the Koreans whom he was kneeling before. As he prayed, his body shook like a jackhammer. It was deeply moving and powerful. Cathe and I had never experienced reconciliation except in the political arena. This was beyond our imaginations, and we were exhilarated.

At the same time, other vignettes of reconciliation from different people groups were taking place. The approximately 500 people attending from all around the world heard about what God was doing with reconciliation. Representatives from several nations shared about experiencing revival connected with prayer and reconciliation. Bishop Joseph Garlington,[4] a Black pastor from Pittsburg, Pennsylvania, led worship and then taught on "Unholy Alliances"—the need to be careful about whom we align ourselves with. Bishop Garlington pointed out, "Louis Farrakhan didn't care anything about those men he called to Washington, D. C. for the Million Man March. He just needed their bodies. It's just like you. The Republican Party doesn't care about you. They just need your bodies." Oh my, when he said that, my heart started pounding. *Oh no, Lord. You're going to make me do something in front of all these people I don't know!*

Repenting on Behalf of the Christian Right

As soon as Bishop Garlington finished, I went to the front and asked if I could reconcile with him. He looked at Ed Silvoso who had convened the meeting. Although I had never heard of him, Ed gave an affirmative nod. I got on my knees and took my Christian Coalition name tag out of my pocket and pinned it on my red blazer. I repented on behalf of my grandfather who had been a member of the Ku Klux Klan and on behalf of other White racists. As Field Director for TXCC, I also repented on behalf of Christian conservatives for our insensitivity, our pride and our sometimes-dogmatic attitudes. I didn't repent for our beliefs, our values, or our work in the public arena. I repented for the angry face some Christians portray when speaking about national issues. Bishop Garlington acknowledged my repentance. He smiled and admitted to being a Republican himself as he graciously forgave me.

Cathe and I ordered the tapes for all the sessions we'd missed. I immediately pursued getting information about Harvest Evangelism, Ed Silvoso's organization, including a phone number. While in LA, I noticed the name of Dave Thompson on his Harvest Evangelism name tag. When I got back to Texas, I called and left a message on Dave Thompson's voice mail.

We discovered that Ed Silvoso has a global vision to fulfill the Great Commission (See Matthew 28:19–20). Ed and his team work to instill vision for city, regional, and nationwide transformation. At the time I met Ed in 1995, he had written only one book, *That None Should Perish*. However, since then he has authored other books including *Prayer Evangelism, Anointed for Business,* and *Transformation*. He began his *city reaching* experiment in Resistencia, Argentina, and has since expanded the concept of *city transformation* around the globe. Ed is recognized in the *prayer movement* as the premier authority on blessing the lost, as well as city and national transformation. He also equips ordinary Christians as *marketplace ministers* wherever they work or go to school.

A couple of weeks after I returned home from LA '95, I got a telephone call from Ed Silvoso himself. He said, "We just watched the video of what you did at our conference. When you mentioned that you worked for Christian Coalition, I thought I'd made a mistake. But I was deeply moved when you humbled yourself and repented. I wept when it happened, and I wept this morning with my staff after watching the video. I asked, 'Who is this woman and how do we contact her?' Dave said that you had called and left your number. Alice, I want you to know that what you did was one of the most important things that happened while we were in Los Angeles. I'm making this organization available to you. Whatever you need, we will do. We'll travel to Texas to talk about how important reconciliation is. I'm sending you two books—my book, *That None Should Perish*, and John Dawson's book, *Healing America's Wounds*. Let me know how we can serve you."

Welcome to the Transformation Movement

Ed invited me to attend his School of Associates in San José, California, in January. I told him I'd try to be there. In the meantime, the tapes we'd ordered in Los Angeles had arrived. At the same time the Executive Director of TXCC suggested that I take two weeks off because I was on the verge of burnout. The tapes from LA '95 arrived during those two weeks and were the perfect thing to fill my time.

As I listened to Ed Silvoso, John Dawson, Jack Hayford, Cindy Jacobs, and other gifted teachers share about a vision to see entire cities reached for Christ using reconciliation, unity, and revival as tools, God began to move on my heart. By the time the School of Associates arrived, I had decided to resign my job and work full time to see Texas reached for Christ. I shared my plans with Ed. He asked me not to resign because he saw Christian Coalition as a powerful vehicle for reconciliation.

Ed was probably right. However, 1996 was a presidential election year. My time would be allocated for elections, precinct conventions, and political party organizing. I had organized 175 county chapters that demanded oversight. I had been highly motivated to organize grassroots in Texas for five years, but now my heart and passion were no longer in political organizing.

At the end of the School of Associates, Ed commissioned me to *reach the state of Texas*. He asked a few leaders to lay hands on me as he prayed a prayer to set me apart for the work in Texas. The snapshot someone gave me later shows three sets of Black hands on my shoulders. Charles Doolittle, the police officer who had repented before the Korean couple at LA '95, his wife Lashanor, and a friend of theirs laid hands on me to set me apart for the work. I didn't know it then, but God would later send me to Black America.

Goodbye Politics–Hello City Reaching

The door to the political arena was shut. I slammed it on my way out. I turned 180 degrees to the vision of reaching entire cities for Christ. I explored signing on as a missionary with Ed Silvoso and Harvest Evangelism. However, at that time Harvest required their missionaries to focus only on their home city, *their Jerusalem*. My heart was not just for Odessa but for the entire state of Texas. Harvest Evangelism's city projects were called *Pray* Something; i.e., *Pray the Bay, Pray*

Simi Valley, etc. The *Pray* before the name designated a *city reaching vision*. The target was pastors praying together across denominational and racial lines with the goal of seeing their city transformed. When I went to San José, *Pray Texas* was in my heart. Since I didn't know what I was doing, I prayed, "Lord, where do I start?"

"Build relationships with leaders." Pastors and key leaders became my target.

I invited Ed to come to Texas and meet with pastors and leaders in Odessa, Big Spring, and Dallas. When Ed walked into the meeting room at the Baptist Building in Odessa where the Pray Texas office was, he was amazed. "The presence of God is here!" Yes, intercessors had prepared the room with worship and prayer. The Lord brought fifteen pastors from various denominations and ethnicities to receive a vision that Odessa could be transformed.

Ed shared his simple strategy. "Come together in unity. Repent for any division. Pray together and invite the Presiding Jesus to lead you." Ed invited the pastors to set their sights on the lost in their city. He expounded from Luke 10 and the Lord's instructions when he sent the 70 out two by two to the cities to prepare the way for Him to visit at a later time. Ed's strategy is called *prayer evangelism*. The foundation for the strategy is Luke 10:1-9.

> Come together in unity. Repent for any division. Pray together and invite the Presiding Jesus to lead you.

- Pray to the Lord of the harvest to send out laborers (verse 2).
- Get out of the Church into the field. You're sent as lambs to wolves (verse 3).

- Speak peace to every house you enter. Release a blessing (verses 5-6).

- Fellowship with the people (even if they are wolves), eating whatever is set before you (verses 7–8).

- Pray for the *felt needs* of the people (verse 9). Their real need is to receive the Lord, but they think their need is for healing, deliverance or provision. Ask the Lord to meet their perceived or *felt needs*. Become transporters of God's blessing, opening your eyes to the needs of people. Some people call this *power evangelism* because you're asking the Lord for miracles. When God performs a miracle, which He loves to do for the lost, they realize how good, compassionate, and powerful the Lord is. They realize how much He loves them when they don't deserve it, and they want to know Him personally.

- Finally say, "The kingdom of God is come near you" (Luke 10:9). Jesus Christ is the One who met your needs. Do you want to know Him?"

Prayer Evangelism

I remember vividly how Ed's teaching turned my paradigm upside down. Formerly, when someone asked me for prayer, I always asked, "Do you know Jesus Christ as your Savior?" I didn't believe the Lord would answer prayers for an unbeliever. I thought you had to be saved before you could get a miracle from the Lord. But just the opposite is true. First, you introduce the Lord by introducing the person to the power of answered prayer, and then they want to know Him. How wrong—judgmental and pharisaical—I had been.

Lord, forgive me. Make me a vessel of blessing and prayer for the lost.

Until I met Ed Silvoso, I didn't have a heart for the lost. I grew up in the Baptist church, which emphasized evangelism. I would go out *witnessing* with the faithful on Monday nights, not because I loved the lost but because it was what I was supposed to do as a faithful church member. My prayer was, "Please don't let anybody be home." I was shy and uncomfortable one on one. But when I learned about prayer evangelism, it changed my life. I no longer had to be able to creatively open a conversation and quickly turn it to evangelism. I could just bless people. Sometimes that meant praying over someone that their needs would be met. And sometimes it just meant saying *God bless you* to people I met who needed to know someone cares about them. It's encouraging to see faces light up when you bless people. Try it yourself. It's liberating!

Georgia Lamothe, a county coordinator with TXCC, invited me to Monahans, a small West Texas town 20 miles west of our home in Odessa. I was able to speak about a vision to reach Monahans to six pastors, both White and Hispanic. "Pray together once a week and ask the Lord to show you how to reach Monahans." The reception by these pastors was overwhelming and they began to pray together once a week. They also started doing prayer initiatives and evangelistic outreaches as the Lord gave them direction. It's true what they say in politics, *The definition of an expert is someone from out of town carrying a briefcase.* I found that to be true. At that time I really didn't know what I was doing, but the pastors I spoke with treated me like an expert. God was opening doors. I was sharing my heart for unity with a vision to reach cities, and God was doing the rest.

When Ed Silvoso came to Odessa, Big Spring and Dallas, the presence of God showed up everywhere we went. Ann Quest, Texas Coordinator for the National Day of Prayer, facilitated the invitation to Dallas leaders. About 50 people came to the prayer chapel at Hillcrest Church in Dallas for the purpose of Ed releasing a vision for the Dallas/Fort Worth Metroplex to be reached for Christ. Pastors and marketplace leaders from various ethnicities, denominations and regions repented to each other. God connected hearts in His presence. Faith was born that their city and region could be transformed if we would pray, seek the Lord together and do whatever He showed us to do. That began my prayer evangelism journey. The Lord opened doors with pastors across Texas.

---

[1] Ed Silvoso, Founder and President of Harvest Evangelism and also of the International Transformation Network (ITN), is widely recognized as a missions strategist and solid Bible teacher who specializes in marketplace transformation. He pioneered the area of city and nation transformation, including blessing the lost, whom he calls *certified sinners*. He has authored *That None Should Perish*, *Prayer Evangelism*, *Anointed for Business*, *Women: God's Secret Weapon* and *Transformation — Change the Markektplace* and *You Change the World*. http://www.harvestevan.org.

[2] BBC News, *Flashback: Rodney King and the LA Riots*, July 10, 2002, http://news.bbc.co.uk/1/hi/world/americas/2119943.stm.

[3] Cindy Jacobs, a prophet and leader, and her husband Mike co-founded Generals International. She has been honored with two Doctorates: Doctor of Divinity from Christian International in Santa Rosa Beach, FL., and from the Asian Theological Association for her work with unreached peoples. She has authored *Possessing the Gates of the Enemy*, *The Voice of God*, *Women of Destiny*, *Deliver Us from Evil*, *The Supernatural Life* and *The Reformation Manifesto*.

[4] Bishop Joseph L. Garlington, Sr., PhD is the Senior Pastor of Covenant Church of Pittsburgh, a multiracial and cross-cultural community of more than two thousand members, which he founded with his wife, Barbara, in 1971. Guided by Bishop Garlington's vision, Covenant Church has been a model of reconciliation and racial healing for Reconciliation Ministries International.

Chapter 3

CLAIMING TERRITORY

PASTOR RICK GILLIS FROM CHRISTIAN LIFE CHURCH in Temple, Texas, called me one day and asked if I would lead a time of prayer at the geographical center of Texas. With satellite technology, it had just been discovered where the precise geographical center of Texas is. Before 1997, Texas only had Spanish maps with the approximate location noted on the map. With the new technology, a marble marker recently had been erected with a three-inch brass star and dot in the middle of it. The dot was the exact geographical center of Texas. The caretakers of the ranch where the monument was located were Christians who realized the significance of what had just been done on the property they were entrusted with.

Opening the Gates of Texas to the King of Glory

Pastor Rick knew there should be prayer there, but he didn't feel he had the network to pull it off. On Saturday, October 25, 1997, seventy of us from across Texas met on the isolated hillside near the tiny town of Rochelle, Texas. Connection was made to the Internet by cell phone as people from ten different nations agreed with us in prayer for Texas. Various people took the cell phone and repented for racism, pride, the lack of love for the lost, and for many other things. A teenage girl cried out to the Lord for her generation. It was powerful. We poured oil on the star on the monument and staked a banner reading, *Jesus Is Lord Over Texas.* We repented. We worshipped. And God opened the heavens that day over our state as we opened the gates of Texas to the King of Glory.

It felt like we were taking baby steps because we didn't have a clear plan for what we were doing, but God was doing amazing things. We began to practice the principles of prayer evangelism that Ed Silvoso taught us from Luke 10. The Lord was sending us out as sheep among wolves. We were *blessing wolves.* One instance of praying blessing prayers happened almost by accident. On a Saturday afternoon in Odessa, we had gathered the pastors and prayer leaders of the city to *stake the city.* We had prepared wooden stakes with *Jesus Is Lord Over Odessa* painted in red on one side and scriptures on the other. A pastor and an intercessor met at each gate—all the highway or railway entrances to Odessa. Representatives of every ethnic group in Odessa joined in. With synchronized timing, pastors and intercessors were repenting and worshipping at the entrances to open the gates of Odessa to the King of Glory. It was a powerful time.

When my husband John, Cathe, my spiritual daughter, Heather and I returned to our office at the Baptist building, we noticed that we had some stakes left over. We decided to go to the building adjacent to our parking lot where the only abortionist in town had an office. Catholic ladies had picketed that office every Tuesday morning for the previous ten years or so. We were pro-life but had never picketed. Neither had we prayed for the abortionist. We knew the office was there, and we didn't like it, but we didn't do anything about it. But that day was different.

We—on the spur of the moment—decided we'd take a couple of leftover stakes and stake out that office. The parking lot and office building were empty because it was a Saturday afternoon. John hammered a stake at both ends of the building in flowerbeds, completely burying the stakes.

Blessing an Abortionist

Then we went to the outside windows of the abortionist's office and began to speak blessings over him. I know. It sounds crazy. *Why would you bless someone who kills babies?* Because the Lord tells us, "Love your enemies, do good to those who hate you, bless those who curse you, pray for those who mistreat you" (Luke 6:27–28). And in Luke 10:3 the Lord sent seventy disciples out *as lambs in the midst of wolves.* The instruction was to say, "Peace be to this house" (verse 5). He said, "If a man of peace is there, your peace will rest upon him; but if not, it will return to you" (verse 6). In other words, speak peace to whoever is in the house. If a lamb is there, your blessing will stay with him. If a wolf is there, the blessing will return to you.

Since blessing an abortionist is probably stretching your mind and your biblical understanding, here's one more scripture to consider. Paul exhorts believers:

> Love without hypocrisy. Abhor what is evil; cling to
> what is good…. Bless those who persecute you; bless
> and curse not…. Never pay back evil for evil to any-
> one. Respect what is right in the sight of all men. If
> possible, so far as it depends on you, be at peace

with all men. Never take your own revenge, beloved,
but leave room for the wrath of God, for it is written,
"Vengeance is Mine, I will repay," says the Lord.
"But if your enemy is hungry, feed him, and if he is
thirsty, give him a drink; for in so doing you will
heap burning coals upon his head." Do not be overcome by evil, but overcome evil with good.
(Romans 12:9-21)

The Word of God is clear—although most of us have never
thought about it in this context. The Lord's instructions concerning evil
people doing evil things is to bless our enemies and to leave room for
the vengeance of God. He didn't say that vengeance was not appropriate. He just said that *our* vengeance was out of line. Our responsibility
is to *bless*. God's responsibility is to *judge*. In fact, verse 21 says that
good overcomes evil and if we are good to our enemies, we heap burning
coals upon the heads of our enemies.

> **PRINCIPLE:** When we are obedient to bless people, the Lord
> causes the blessing to remain—if the person we're blessing is
> a man of peace. If we bless those who are not worthy of the
> blessing, our blessing releases God's dealings in their lives.

We blessed the abortionist in every way we could think of. We
worshipped. We shouted. We lifted up the Name of Jesus over that
place. We gave Him jurisdiction on the property and in the lives of
those in the building—including a man who snuffed out the lives of
little babies before they were born.

When I think of how loud we were that day, it makes me smile. The Lord gave us a time and place where we were free to worship and to bless. Our worship was fun. It never occurred to us that something profoundly spiritual was taking place until a couple of months later when Heather came into the office with some incredible news.

God Proves Himself Mighty

The owner of the building told Heather's dad, who was his friend, that he had kicked the abortionist out of the building for nonpayment of rent!!! We were stunned. And we knew what happened. God had taken possession of the property we had staked in His name and used those blessing prayers for His purposes. Several years later the man faced charges of tax fraud and ended up in prison! That's the last I heard about him. We blessed the man, and God pronounced judgment upon him.

> **PRINCIPLE:** There is something about actually staking territory. You give the Lord jurisdiction over land and regions by staking land.

The Lord wants to possess nations. We can help by giving Him little pieces of territory. Isaiah 54:2-3 says:

> Enlarge the place of your tent. Stretch out the curtains of your dwellings, spare not. Lengthen your cords and strengthen your pegs. For you will spread abroad to the right and to the left and your descendants will possess nations, and they will resettle the desolate cities.

God Opens Door to Democratic State Convention

The second place where we put prayer evangelism principles to the test was at the Democratic State Convention in Dallas in 1996. Okay. Just relax and read the story. Although TXCC was made up mostly of Republicans, the Texas State Chairman had tried to rent a booth at the Democratic State Convention in both 1992 and 1994. The Texas Democratic Party always refused. However, in 1996—just as we were learning about the power of blessing—the Democrats said TXCC could have a booth. I had already resigned as Field Director, but Cathe was still Training Director. *And* Cathe was also a Democrat. It was hard for her to remain a Democrat after she became pro-life, but she was hanging in there. Since Cathe was a delegate to the convention, she could legally ask for a caucus—a meeting at the convention for TXCC! So they had a booth and an approved caucus!

About 30 people attended the caucus—all Democrats except for Ann Quest, Janie McKay and me who were there to pray. Cathe opened with prayer and shared the vision of TXCC, including their desire to work with Democrats and to work for moral values in both parties. In the room were a couple of pro-life Hispanics, some Jews wearing their yarmulkes, some people who were quiet that we couldn't identify, several homosexuals, and Emma Warren—a delegate, prayer warrior, and member of the Bexar County Christian Coalition in San Antonio. Emma was one of very few members of a local Christian Coalition chapter who was both Black and a Democrat.

The homosexuals in the caucus were the most vocal. A young heavy-set lesbian asked Cathe, "What do you really think about me?"

Cathe responded, "I believe you are made in God's image, and I love you. It's not you as a person that I oppose. It's your political agenda I disagree with." Cathe spoke the truth with grace and compassion. Her anointed words broke through the atmosphere of suspicion, fear, and anger. Something happened in the spirit because the TXCC booth, a front for a *prayer evangelism* operation of *blessing the lost and praying for their felt needs,* became the *place to be for homosexuals.* Two handsome young men stopped by the booth and said, "Thank you for not hating us. We're Christians, too." They told us that they attended an Episcopalian church in Tyler. We were shocked, but were not there to straighten out anyone's theology. We were there to bless.

> "I believe you are made in God's image, and I love you. It's not you as a person that I oppose. It's your political agenda I disagree with."

The Holy Spirit was drawing homosexuals to the booth to get blessed. I wish I could tell you that we learned later that these young men and women left the *gay lifestyle* and were totally set free. I can't tell you that. The Lord let us know what happened to the abortionist, but we heard nothing after the Democratic Convention. I pray that God is still dealing with their hearts and that they will find freedom in Jesus Christ one day.

Surprising Invitation

In the spring of 1998 I got a call from my friend, Susan Weddington. Susan served on my Pray Texas Board of Directors and had attended many meetings and retreats we had convened with pastors and leaders. Susan informed me that the Chairman of the Republican Party of Texas had just resigned, and as Vice Chairman she had automatically become Chairman. The Republican State Convention was coming up in June. Susan asked if I would organize a prayer rally and bring a team of intercessors to pray for the convention.

I wasn't interested. I had closed the political door. My rejection from a leader who wouldn't work with me because of my political past was still fresh on my mind. But Susan was persistent. "I don't care what you do. I just want the presence of God there."

"Can it be about reconciliation?"

"Anything—as long as God's presence is there."

Having a special time of prayer was nothing new at Texas Republican State Conventions. Before Susan's administration, *prayer breakfasts* (with no food) were held but not well attended. Less than 100 people generally showed up. The ecumenical program consisted of priests, rabbis, and pastors reading their prayers plus a dry, boring speaker. The presence of God was nowhere near the place. Susan, however, wanted to publicize the prayer rally to all the convention delegates and alternates as a time of worship and prayer with a personal invitation from her. Was the Lord opening this door?

Revealing Satan's Lie

I accepted Susan's carte blanche offer and began organizing the prayer rally for the last day of the convention, Saturday, June 13, 1998, at 7:30 A.M. at the Tarrant County Convention Center, Fort Worth. I asked Ruben Duarte,[1] worship leader and also Pray Texas board member and now pastor of The Life Center in San Antonio, to lead worship. Pastor Ruben understands, more than anyone I've ever met, how to lead people into God's presence with praise and exaltation, how to move into adoration—and how to stay there. I asked two Black leaders, Dr. Walter Fletcher,[2] then associate pastor at Hillcrest Church in

Dallas, and Pastor Ron O'Guinn, former Reconciliation Director for Promise Keepers and head of AllOfUs in Grapevine, to pray. Two Hispanic pastors, Dan Aleman, pastor of Creek Crossing Harvest Church in Mesquite, and Ramiro Peña, pastor of Christ the King Church in Waco, plus Messianic Jewish Rabbi Marty Cohen were also scheduled to pray. All were instructed to pray as the Lord leads. My role would be to guide the process and, of course, to share my heart about racism, repentance, and reconciliation. The plan was to worship the Lord, repent for racism, and openly appreciate and honor each other.

Even as I made plans for the rally and prayer teams that would be deployed at the convention, I harbored a nagging feeling that I was getting off track from what the Lord called me to do. Here I was back in the political arena—even though it was for prayer and reconciliation. I mistakenly thought the perfect context for my work was pastors and churches in a spiritual setting. That is until I drove into Fort Worth.

Brutal Murder in Jasper

I turned on the radio and heard the horrible news about the murder of Black American James Byrd, Jr. of Jasper. Remember? Three White guys—young adults—tied Mr. Byrd to the back of a pickup truck and dragged him through the woods to his death. I later drove down the lonely single-lane paved road in the piney woods of Deep East Texas. Orange circles designated the spots where Mr. Byrd's dismembered body parts had been scattered.

I was shocked! It might not have been so astounding if the murder had been in Alabama, Georgia, Mississippi, Louisiana, or another state in the Deep South. But it happened in Texas! The Lord said, "This is a Texas sin. Are you going to own it?"

Instantly I knew why I was leading the prayer rally at the Republican State Convention. God wanted public acknowledgment of racism and a public, corporate apology.

A couple of months earlier at Eddie Smith's PrayUSA meeting in Houston, I sat at lunch next to a pastor from Kirbyville, Texas. Since I've organized so much by county, when I meet someone from a town I don't recognize, I ask what county they're from. Pastor Charles Burchett of First Baptist Church in Kirbyville told me he lived in Jasper County.

Upon hearing the news of Mr. Byrd's murder in Jasper, I immediately thought of Pastor Charles. I telephoned and asked if he would come to Fort Worth and repent on behalf of the White church in Jasper for the murder of James Byrd, Jr. and for the mindsets that breed hatred throughout Texas.

Pastor Charles responded, "My heart says *yes*, but I've learned to pray about these things. Call me in the morning and I'll give you my answer." When I called him the next morning, I hardly recognized his voice. He was deathly ill. He said, "If I have to crawl there, I'll be there." What happened at the prayer rally was unbelievable!

---

[1] Rev. Ruben Duarte is Senior Pastor of The Life Center Christian Fellowship, San Antonio, Texas. An accomplished musician and song writer, he produced the worship CD, *MagniFire*.

[2] Dr. Walter Fletcher and his wife Deede co-founded Desert Rivers International. Dr. Fletcher is the author of *Recovering the Soul: A Call to Spiritual Health*. He serves as a pastor, teacher and adjunct professor.

Chapter 4

THE PRESENCE OF GOD IN THE POLITICAL ARENA

WORSHIP GREETED THE ALMOST 2,000 PEOPLE who streamed into the auditorium at 7:30 A.M. on Saturday. A personal invitation in each delegate packet announced a time of worship, prayer, and repentance. The presence of God overwhelmed us. People worshipped with passion and repented with genuine brokenness. The Holy Spirit was stronger than anything I had experienced in any church or spiritual meeting.

After the worship I shared about the murder of Mr. James Byrd, Jr. and what God had told me about this being a Texas sin. I don't remember exactly what I said, but I do remember how quiet it was and the impact on the audience. I gave the platform to the various pastors to pray. Everything they said was profound and important.

Pastor Charles Burchett, tall and lanky at 6'4", bent over on his hands and knees with his head touching the floor. He wept. And he wept! He wept over the sin of racism in the church, in Jasper, in Texas, and in America. In addition to specific repentance for racism, hatred, pride, and ignorance in the White church, Pastor Charles prayed,

"Dear God, place the spirit of Antichrist under the feet of Jesus. Forgive the White church in Texas for its sin."

We cried out together for God to heal our land. While Pastor Charles prayed as a representative of the White church, Dr. Fletcher prayed as a representative of the Black community by responding with forgiveness and repentance.

At the end of the rally, Susan took the microphone for the first time, "As Chairman of the Republican Party of Texas and by the authority invested in this office, I open this Party to the presence of Almighty God." I was amazed as another wave of the Holy Spirit moved in. I don't think that Susan realized the implications of what she'd done. She didn't think about it in advance. She just did what God directed her to do on the spot. It was powerful!

Intercessors, dispersed throughout the convention to practice *prayer evangelism* by praying and blessing, had many divine encounters. The anointing of the Holy Spirit was heavy each time an intercessor prayed. Susan asked my husband John, a seasoned, mature prayer warrior, to serve as her personal intercessor. It was incredible to watch John take his post as a watchman and a protector. His gifts of wisdom and discernment were in full operation in that role. If you're a man, be encouraged! Strong men are taking their places as watchmen and intercessors. Why do we leave spiritual warfare to women? We shouldn't.

People often would mistake the name of our ministry, Pray Texas, to think I was an intercessor and that Pray Texas would be an intercessory ministry. It wasn't. It was a city-reaching ministry founded upon reconciliation and a desire to welcome the presence of God into cities for social transformation. My husband John is the intercessor in the family. He's also the one with the most discernment. I do pray—so please don't reprimand me for not being an intercessor—but the burden to lift people up in prayer is not as strong on me as it is on John. I'm more of a connector and catalyst. But we need intercessors—both men and women—to prepare the way in prayer.

Intercessors Released

Susan's designated authority empowered the intercessors to move at a higher level than they had ever experienced before. A partnership between intercessors and government leaders was birthed. It was pioneered in the political arena. Currently in the marketplace intercessors are connecting with CEOs. Business leaders are asking for intercessors to pray for them, their staffs, and their businesses. It's working in the marketplace like we have seen it work in the political arena.

As a political activist, I had attended several large meetings convened at the State Republican Convention by various *pro-family* organizations, including TXCC. The media would always be there filing very negative reports. They would emphasize some in the audience with raised hands and would describe the gatherings with derogatory phrases like *tent revivals*, etc. They tried to characterize Christians in the civic arena as religious *weirdos*. But something was different at the prayer rally.

> **PRINCIPLE:** When the presence of God is in the room, everyone is touched.

The media came, of course. But there were no disparaging reports. In fact, the *Houston Chronicle* printed only one small paragraph about the gathering, quoting Pastor Charles' repentance and the prayer he had prayed about the Antichrist. Why?

First, at the TXCC statewide conference, and now at the prayer rally at the Republican Convention, the media had given a good report. More hand-raising and shouts of "Hallelujah!" than at previous pro-family events had taken place, but those things weren't reported. The presence of God had saturated the room and touched the hearts of the media as well as every delegate in the room.

> The presence of God had saturated the room and touched the hearts of the media as well as every delegate in the room.

Revealing Satan's Lie

A few weeks after the convention, I met Dave Thompson of Harvest Evangelism at a March for Jesus meeting in Austin. "Dave, you won't believe it! The presence of God was so strong and came so easily. The few intercessors we'd recruited came ready for spiritual warfare. We expected great resistance, but there was none. It was so easy to pray at the political convention—much easier than in church!"

He replied, "That's the lie of the enemy to make us think that God only shows up in church. The Lord wants to demonstrate His power and presence in the secular arena outside the four walls of the church."

Then I understood why Ed Silvoso had wanted me to stay with TXCC. The political arena needs reconciliation and transformation. Even though I had shut the door on the political arena, the Lord re-opened it in His time and in His way.

Susan received only good reports from the delegates who had attended the prayer rally. It was the beginning of people wanting to be delegates to the state convention so they could attend the prayer rally. People from every denomination and every region in the state, as well as different ethnicities, attended. Everyone was blessed. Repentance, fervent prayer, and expressive worship were at the forefront. Why weren't people uncomfortable?

> **PRINCIPLE:** Repentance and the presence of God are the determining factors in how people of diverse backgrounds, cultures and theological expressions receive what is happening. The power of the Spirit of God overwhelms all differences.

God was pioneering a model in Texas. Later I was taught the concept of welcoming the presence of God into your sphere of influence. You can do that in your home, in your office, in your club or as Susan did, into a political party. We get so focused on what we're there to do—in our business or club. But God wants to be invited into our lives and spheres.

> **PRINCIPLE:** You can invite the Holy Spirit into your sphere of authority. All it takes is a welcome from someone on the inside. Welcome Him now into your home, your business, your classroom, or wherever you are.

When the prayer rally was over, I thought that was the end. But it was just the beginning. What God did in Houston in 2002 was off the charts! I'll share that later.

Meanwhile, before the Republican State Convention was to be held in Houston in June 2000, Susan had started to research the history of the Republican Party of Texas. She found some astounding information. She called me with the news that Blacks and abolitionists had founded the Texas Republican Party. The first Republican State Convention was held in Houston in 1867 with 150 Black delegates and 20 Whites! Susan asked, "What happened? We have to know what happened. Where are our Black leaders?" She called David Barton of WallBuilders[1] and asked him to do research to discover what happened. Although Susan believed in reconciliation, I was the one pushing the reconciliation agenda at the prayer rallies. Now Susan was deeply moved and motivated on the racism issue.

The Racial Track in the Political Arena

The Lord had us on this track—this *racial track* right in the middle of the political arena. What was He doing? Susan again asked me to organize the prayer rally and the intercessory prayer team for the 2000 convention. I knew we were to find out what the sins and the breaches were under the six flags that had flown over Texas during its history. *What did we need to repent for under the flags of Spain, France, Mexico, the Republic of Texas, the Confederacy, and the United States?* I asked Pastor Charles to head up the intercessory teams and orchestrate the prayer rally ceremonies.

As intercessors began to pray many weeks before the convention, one of them envisioned Susan pouring oil on bricks. So we started looking for bricks. Susan wanted to meet privately in front of the George R. Brown Convention Center in Houston and pray about whatever caused Black Republicans to walk away from the political party they had founded in that city. I called Doug Stringer in Houston, founder of Somebody Cares America, and he sent two Black ministers from his staff. Tim and Joyce James, pastors of Total Man Christian Ministries in Houston, a mostly Black congregation and formerly on my Pray Texas board, came as well. It was a small group. We met in a little park right across the street from the convention center. Lo and behold, there were the bricks!

We worshipped. The presence of God came. When it came time for Susan to pour the oil on the bricks as the intercessor had visualized, Susan surprised me. I thought she would ask forgiveness for whatever White Republicans did to drive Blacks away from their party, but instead she prayed, "Lord, I forgive our leaders for walking away. And I open the door and invite them back in." Remember that, because two years later God did a miracle in a Black pastor from Houston, Dr. C. L. Jackson, and that set us on a new course.

Repentance for Iniquities Under the Six Flags of Texas

The prayer rally that year was amazing. Pastor Charles had put together a team of spiritual mappers including Bill and Connie Fisher of Houston and Cathe Halford of Odessa to research the history of Texas under the six flags. Then we found people to represent the various countries. Marcie Rea from Amarillo is a descendant of Spanish Conquistador Cabeza de Vaca. She dressed up like Queen Isabella of Spain. Marcie repented to a Sephardic Jew, a Jew of Spanish descent, for expelling the Jews in 1492. That's right! The year 1492 was when *Columbus sailed the ocean blue* and Queen Isabella expelled the Jews from Spain. Although they were forced to be Catholics, the Jews wouldn't stop celebrating their feasts and lighting their Shabbat candles. Many historians believe that Christopher Columbus was actually a Sephardic Jew who had converted to Christianity, and many who traveled with him in those first ships were Jews fleeing persecution.

> Many historians believe that Christopher Columbus was actually a Sephardic Jew who had converted to Christianity, and many who traveled with him in those first ships were Jews fleeing persecution.

Pastor Edsel Dureus,[2] dressed in French garb, repented for denominational division. The King of France had declared that France was the *most Christian* versus the King of Spain saying that Spain was the *most Catholic*.

Pastor Ramiro Peña, dressed as a Mexican president, repented to Heather Holder who was part Native American for mistreating the natives. Bill Fisher, a descendant of the first Treasurer of Texas, dressed as a Confederate general. He repented to Emma Warren, a descendant from slaves, for racism and not honoring Blacks. I'll never forget the sight of Emma's Black hand on the shoulder of that Confederate uniform as Bill and Emma knelt together in worship. It was powerful.

A former freemason from Oklahoma, dressed as a Texas pioneer wearing a Masonic apron, repented for freemasonry. As he repented, he took off the apron and threw it to the ground. He declared, "Stephen F. Austin is not the father of Texas. Lord, You are!" The 2,000 plus people at the Republican Prayer Rally stood to their feet and shouted!

Under the United States flag, Tim McCall, a medical doctor from Waco, repented for the shedding of innocent blood on our land through abortion. As the former owner of an abortion clinic, Carol Everett, founder of a pro-life organization called The Heidi Group in

Austin, repented on behalf of women who have had abortions. She voiced a prayer of healing and forgiveness for them.

The prayer rally was beautiful, but it was also powerful. With the backdrop of worship, the two people dressed in the attire of the day came down the aisle following the flag they were representing. The offending parties, Queen Isabella, king of France, president of Mexico, Confederate general, Stephen F. Austin and American citizen knelt before the parties they had offended—a Sephardic Jew, a slave, a Native American and a woman—and expressed a specific and precise prayer of repentance. The offended parties responded with forgiveness. As they finished their portion on the program, they went down on one knee with their backs to the audience. When the repentance was finished, in came a banner, *King of kings*. At that point everyone on stage went down prostrate upon their faces as the audience sang, "Lord, take up Your holy throne throughout all this land. Take the place that is Yours alone, throughout all this land. And of the increase of Your government, there will be no end. There will be no end. There will be no end. You are worthy, Lord, to reign!"[3]

Everyone in the audience was on their feet worshipping the Lord, exalting Him and giving Him extravagant praise. We celebrated the King of kings together.

Coming in the Opposite Spirit

At the end of the rally, I went to the microphone and shared about the mantle of humility. One of the most powerful spiritual weapons we have is coming in the opposite spirit. I led the audience in prayer asking the Lord to mantle us with humility while coming in the opposite spirit prevalent in the political arena—pride, ambition, and competition.

> **PRINCIPLE:** When we come in the opposite spirit, such as humility instead of pride in the political arena, it's a powerful weapon against the enemy. Humility overcomes pride, arrogance and ambition. Light dispels darkness. Mercy overcomes judgment. A blessing is more powerful than a curse. Humility disarms pride. Coming in the opposite spirit is one of the most important weapons that we can exercise.

Not only did we welcome the Lord, repent, and worship Him, but we also exited the prayer rally mantled with God's character and the scent of His presence for the last day of the convention.

That year a large team of intercessors was led by Pastor Charles, a gifted delegator and administrator. He assigned Cathe to lead the prayerwalking teams. The teams were dispatched to the various committees. Charles was connected to the leadership and security by walkie-talkies. Any time a team of intercessors would be needed at any place in the convention, word was relayed to Charles and he dispatched the teams. The power of partnership between the spheres of government and the church was evident.

Along with the prayer rally and prayer teams, Susan set aside a *ministry room* headed up by Pastor Ramiro. Susan asked him to staff the room with pastors that he trusted who were capable of ministering to any need a convention attendee might have.

As a result of Susan's directive to prepare a place of ministry and dispatching intercessors at the convention, God answered many prayers. A security guard received ministry. A homeless man found a job. Charles got a call from security that Black Panthers were on their way to the convention center to demonstrate. Security prepared to barricade doors and immediately intercessors cried out to the Lord for His intervention. The demonstrators never showed up!

Choosing Pastors Skilled in Prayer

One of the things Susan asked me to do before all the conventions was to recruit pastors to pray during the convention sessions. With 15,000 or more attending, the Texas Republican Convention is the largest political convention in the United States simply because of the way Texas chooses its delegates. Susan wanted pastors from various ethnicities who knew how to touch heaven and invite the presence of God to pray at the convention. At the Houston convention in 2000, Marty Cohen, a Messianic rabbi, opened the convention with prayer with his *talit*—prayer shawl—covering his head. He prayed in the name of Jesus and then recited the Aaronic Blessing from Numbers 6:24-26 in both English and Hebrew.

> The LORD bless you, and keep you; the LORD make
> His face shine on you, and be gracious to you: the
> LORD lift up His countenance on you, and give you
> peace.

It was powerful—so powerful that a Jewish delegate married to a Baptist man asked to speak to Rabbi Marty and subsequently accepted Jesus as her Savior. Yes, it was a political convention, but God had been there.

Before the 2002 convention that was to be held in Dallas, Susan was praying about the convention in her quiet time. She felt that she was to call Governor Rick Perry for a recommendation of a Black or Hispanic pastor that was close to him to pray at the Republican convention. Immediately Governor Perry replied, "Pastor C. L. Jackson of Pleasant Grove Missionary Baptist Church in Houston." Dr. Jackson[4] was a life-long Democrat, but someone had introduced him to Republican Rick Perry when he was Lt. Governor and they had become friends.

Susan had a staff member call Dr. Jackson to see if he would entertain a call from the Chairman of the Republican Party of Texas. He responded, "Yes." Then Susan called and asked him if he would pray at the convention.

Governor's Friend Welcomed to Pray

"I understand you're a Democrat. Please know that I'm not trying to make you a Republican. I just want to honor one of our Governor's friends." Susan asked Dr. Jackson to pray on Saturday afternoon, after all the party officers—chairman, vice-chairman and 62 members of the State Republican Executive Committee would have been elected. Most pastors were simply asked to pray, but Susan asked Dr. Jackson to first give a charge about leadership to the newly elected party officials as well as to pray over them.

At the Dallas Convention Center, Susan told me about Dr. Jackson. She pointed him out to me and asked me to see if he wanted to pray at the prayer rally the next day—Saturday at 7 A.M. Dr. Jackson said he would be there. He asked me if I wanted him to write out his prayer for approval. I was surprised at the question but assured him that wasn't necessary. He could just pray what the Lord led him to pray.

We would be praying specifically for judges at that prayer meeting. By then, I had started Justice at the Gate to pray for judges because more of our freedoms have been robbed through Supreme Court decisions made by activist judges than by laws enacted through state legislatures or the Congress. Removing prayer from public schools and Roe v. Wade, which struck down every pro-life law in the nation, are two of the most notorious court decisions. I explained to Dr. Jackson that we would be praying for judges and for our nation, and whatever he wanted to pray was fine.

The Saturating Presence of God

Saturday morning came and almost 5,000 people had gathered. Yes! Word continued to spread from year to year about the presence of God and time of genuine prayer and worship at the convention. Many people have told me over the years that they attend Republican State Conventions because they want to be in God's presence at the prayer rallies. Pastor Ruben always led worship. This year Pastor Dan Aleman and Pastor Charles would pray, among others. Two judges, Judge Cynthia Kent from Tyler, and Judge Faith Johnson, first Black Republican judge ever elected in Dallas County, attended. Falma Rufus,[5] my dear sister from the Dallas Metroplex and founder of Pray His Song, sang a prophetic song over the judges. It was powerful! Falma, who is Black, has an incredible gift of singing the song of the Lord. When Falma is teamed up with Ruben on the keyboard, their worshipping hearts spill over to the people in a powerful way. Pastor Dan, Judge Johnson, and I were on our knees on the platform as Falma sang over the judges. Judge Kent was weeping. Judge Johnson had her hands raised as she worshipped on her knees. Do you want to see the government on her knees before the Lord? I've seen it with my own eyes.

Dr. Jackson came into the prayer rally with a small entourage of five or six from East Texas that included pastors and sons in ministry. They were all asked to join Dr. Jackson on the stage. Before he was given the microphone to pray, Pastor Charles prayed. As always, repentance for racism was on our agenda. Pastor Charles was on his knees asking the Lord to forgive us for not honoring and respecting our Black brothers and sisters. He named racism, pride and hypocrisy as only he can. Then he handed the microphone to Dr. Jackson. I don't remember what he prayed, but I do remember what happened later that afternoon.

------

1 David Barton is Founder and President of WallBuilders (www.wallbuilders.com), a national pro-family organization. David is the author of numerous best-selling books, with the subjects being drawn largely from his massive library of tens of thousands of original writings from the Founding Era. He was named by *Time Magazine* as one of America's 25 most influential evangelicals. He has received numerous national and international awards, including Who's Who in Education, the Daughters of the American Revolution's highest award and the George Washington Honor Medal. His work in media has merited several Angel Awards, Telly Awards and the Dove Foundation Seal of Approval.

2 Edsel Dureus is Founder and President of Taking the Word to the World Ministries, Inc. He is pastor of Thanksgiving Tabernacle Bible Fellowship in Cedar Hill, Texas.

3 Rick Ridings, *Lord Take Up Your Holy Throne*, © 1989 Arise Music.

4 Charles L. Jackson was appointed to the Texas Board of Criminal Justice in November 2005 *(Term expires 2/2011)*. Dr. Jackson chairs the Community Corrections Committee and is a member of the Health Care, Rehabilitation and Reentry Programs and Victim Services Committees. He received a Bachelor of Theology Degree from the Baptist Theological Center, Inc. in Houston, Texas. He also received a Doctor of Divinity from The Mount Hope Bible College and a Doctor of Laws from the Union Baptist Bible College and Seminary, both in Houston. Dr. Jackson is the author of eighteen books, the most notable of which is *God's Mouthpiece,* resulting in his induction into the Martin Luther King Hall of Preachers, Morehouse College, Atlanta, Georgia. He has been the Pastor of Pleasant Grove Missionary Baptist Church for 40 years.

5 Falma Rufus is Founder of Pray His Song. Internationally known, she is a gifted psalmist. Falma produced the worship CD, *In the Clouds, An Encounter with Prophetic Psalmist: Falma Rufus.*

Chapter 5

⚜

HEALING HEARTS—
CHANGING LIVES

REPUBLICAN STATE CONVENTION DELEGATES AND ALTERNATES were not accustomed to having Democrats speak or even pray at their conventions. Dr. Jackson was a life-long Democrat. The Who's Who of American politics had been in his church, including Dr. Martin Luther King, Jr., Roselyn Carter, the wife of President Jimmy Carter, and a long line of Democratic candidates and elected officials. In fact, if you wanted to get elected as a Democrat in Houston, it was imperative to attend at least one service at Pleasant Grove Missionary Baptist Church. Susan had made it clear that she knew he was a Democrat, and she wasn't trying to make him a Republican.

Dr. Jackson Stuns the Convention

When Dr. Jackson took the stage before more than 10,000 delegates and alternates, he thanked the *Chair Lady* of the Republican Convention. He spoke about the prayer rally he had attended earlier in the morning and how he'd never *seen anything on that order*. He spoke about getting out the vote. What? Getting out the vote? Then he said,

83

"I came into this convention a Democrat, but I'm leaving a Republican because God is in this place."

Did I hear him right? Did he really say what I think he said? Susan later commented, "I couldn't believe what I was hearing. It was all I could do to keep from falling on my face right there and thanking God."

You can probably imagine that Dr. Jackson became a close friend after that. Today, many years later, he is one of my dearest friends in all the earth. I call him *Dr. J.* and he calls me *Bishop.* After getting to know Dr. Jackson a little better, I asked him what happened to him at the convention to make him change parties.

He said, "First of all, I've never been to a prayer meeting so early. We had to get up about 5 o'clock in the morning to get there. We didn't know what to expect. When we got there, there were already 4,000 people there. I'd never seen it on that order. Then when that White pastor got on his knees and prayed right before me.... When he asked God to forgive Whites for racism—well, I'd never heard a White man pray like that. After the prayer rally, I told the pastors who were with me that we needed to go back to the hotel room and pray. And we did. We got on our knees and started seeking the Lord about everything we had seen and heard."

I asked, "Dr. J., when did you know that you were going to change parties?"

"I didn't know it 'til it came out of my mouth!"

The Magnitude of What God Did

Now take a few minutes and let this sink in. Dr. C. L. Jackson. A man of God then in his sixties who is a spiritual father in Houston. A respected Black pastor who had been in the highest political circles in the nation. He had traveled to Nairobi with President Bill Clinton. Many political leaders had honored him. He was very engaged in elections. In fact, for all elections he has a polling place set up in his church in downtown Houston. I've seen the almost one-inch thick Get Out The Vote (GOTV) Manual for his church. He's very organized. He has a GOTV Coordinator in his choir and in every Sunday school class. He rents buses every year to get out the vote. If you're a Democrat in Houston, you know the influence of Dr. Charles L. Jackson.

Black Ministers Endorse Republican Governor

Do you think Dr. Jackson changed political parties without paying a price? *Think again!* But Dr. Jackson is unafraid. He went back to the Black ministerial alliance in Houston and spoke to the pastors. That alliance is not only a 501(c) 3 organization, they have a Political Action Committee (PAC) that allows them to legally endorse candidates. Knowing how to leverage their influence and effectiveness is nothing new to Black pastors at election time. Susan and I were in a church in Houston when, before the media, about 80 Black pastors formally endorsed Republican Rick Perry for Governor. That was historic.

While the national average is just 9 percent of the Black vote for Republicans, Gov. Rick Perry has been successful in getting 16 percent of the Black vote. Undoubtedly Dr. Jackson's influence had a huge impact on that vote. Dr. Jackson didn't just introduce Houston pastors to Gov. Perry, he also traveled the state to talk with his colleagues.

Dr. Jackson Joins the Team

Soon Dr. Jackson began to travel with us as well. As I mentioned, I had started Justice at the Gate in January 2002. Although praying for judges and voter registration in churches was our dual stated purpose, reconciliation is a part of everything I do. With the divine connection with Dr. Jackson, God began to put together a team—a powerful team. Two years before, Susan had asked David Barton to do research to find out why Black Republicans had left the party they founded. He had been researching for two years and he discovered some astounding facts. David's research is now in both DVD and a book, *Setting the Record Straight—American History in Black and White*.[1]

For instance, the Republican Party on the national level was started by several anti-slavery Democrats who had tired of their party's ardent pro-slavery position. They had a very clearly stated purpose in their founding: to end slavery. The early platform comparisons show the Democrats supporting slavery as well as the Dred Scott Supreme Court decision, which states Blacks were not persons but property. The early platforms of the Republican Party consisted of two issues—ending slavery to give equal rights to Blacks and the support of traditional marriage opposing polygamy. The first national Republican Party platform "was a short document with only nine planks in the platform, but significantly, six of the nine planks set forth bold declarations of equality and civil rights for African Americans based on the principles of the Declaration of Independence."[2]

> The Republican Party on the national level was started by several anti-slavery Democrats who had tired of their party's ardent pro-slavery position.

Another surprising fact that David uncovered was that *the Ku Klux Klan was started by Democrats to oppose Republicans!* Well, that certainly matched my understanding of my grandfather. He was a staunch Democrat and would have disowned any of his family members who voted Republican. Even my dad, who became a Christian immediately before he and mother married in 1941, died a Democrat. One day Dad mused, "I can't figure out how I raised three Republicans!" I replied, "You raised us with your moral values. And the Republican Party lines up with those values." Politics was one subject I tried to avoid. Dad and I would never agree on party affiliation. He was very glad when I left TXCC to start Pray Texas. And he had no idea that I was organizing prayer rallies for Republican conventions.

Meetings with an Agenda

At the end of 2002, Justice at the Gate held a meeting in Dr. Jackson's church. We had an agenda. Worship to invite the presence of God, repent for racism, share Dr. Jackson's testimony, and have David Barton give the truth about American and Black history. This wasn't a Republican meeting even though Susan and David were Republican Party officials. It was a spiritual meeting. And lives were changed.

Our team consisted of Blacks Dr. Jackson and Falma Rufus, Hispanic Ruben Duarte, and Whites David Barton, Susan Weddington, and me. Ruben led us into God's presence with worship. Falma released the prophetic word in song and worshipped along with Ruben. They are powerful together. Susan or I would repent for racism. Dr. Jackson would share his story and give his favor to David. David shared hidden truths about America's spiritual heritage and eye-opening facts about Black History.

At that meeting at Dr. Jackson's church, Falma brought a Black minister with her, Evangelist William Morris from Los Angeles. Falma told him that she was going to Houston for a Justice at the Gate meeting. He asked, "Why are you hanging around those White people?" She welcomed him to come with her and find out.

He came. He found out. God touched William's life in a deep way. He needed to hear a White person repent, even though he wasn't conscious of it. And the truth of history turned his paradigm upside down. "Why aren't we taught these things?" Just as the spiritual history of our nation has been expunged from public school textbooks, Black History has also been omitted or distorted. William was changed. Many more would be as well. We had fallen into a model, a strategy for personal transformation. It wasn't something we planned—it's just something that happened.

Healing Hearts—Changing Lives

At this point, you may have a hard time believing that we weren't trying to change Black Democrats into Republicans, but you'd be wrong. We wanted to see hearts healed, to educate, and to empower. Our goal was to change Black voters into *values* voters and give them *access* to government. But just like Dr. Jackson, many Black Americans who attended these meetings had their hearts healed, received education, and changed political parties. Not all, but many.

Because we have experienced so many meetings where people's lives have been transformed, we have discovered a key.

> PRINCIPLE: Welcoming the presence of God through worship, as well as acknowledging racism and repenting for it, are essential before the facts of history can be presented. Otherwise the wounds from racism drown out the speaker—no matter how powerful the presentation is.

So what happened to Evangelist William Morris? William was touched deep down in his spirit by the presence of God, the repentance, and the information. He became a dear friend and colleague. When William's eyes were opened, he wanted to be a part of opening others' eyes. God connected us because He wants to "loose the bands of wickedness and let the oppressed go free and to break every yoke" (Isaiah 58:12). It happened to William, and it was powerful.

The meeting at Pleasant Grove was small. I thought that more of Dr. Jackson's congregation would be there, but only a few came. Dr. Jackson has paid a price for changing parties and connecting with Republicans. But a few of Dr. Jackson's spiritual sons were there, including Rev. Melvin Lewis. At the end of the meeting Rev. Lewis stepped up to the microphone and began to sing *God Bless America* a cappella. As his rich bass voice filled the sanctuary, we all joined in. We corporately asked God to bless the nation we love—America. I sensed that God was shattering strongholds. We sang our prayer, our love for the Lord and our love for our country. We were united in heart and spirit. God had broken down walls, healed hearts and connected us by His Spirit. It was glorious.

The next morning at breakfast William was still incredulous over what God had done. He was no longer wondering why Falma was hanging out with these White people. He wanted to hang out, too. So after all these things, what did we learn?

> **PRINCIPLE:** God wants us to know our own history as well as our nation's history. Because "Jesus Christ is the same yesterday, today and forever" (Hebrews 13:8), He can deal with the past as though it were today.

Susan's obedience to pray and repent in 2000 in Houston resulted in Houstonian Dr. C. L. Jackson's personal transformation in 2002 with the ripple effect of changing many lives.

> **PRINCIPLE:** Being obedient to do the next thing—no matter how small it is, like pouring oil on brick and praying—can change history.

Think about this fact—you could be one obedient act away from breakthrough. What is the Lord asking you to do? Quickly obey and watch God move on your behalf.

Night of Transformation at Harvest Time Church

The Lord used Dr. Jackson to open doors with Black pastors. He approached Bishop Shelton Bady, the successful pastor of Harvest Time Church in Houston, because he knew Bishop Bady to be a man of the Book who values truth. Bishop Bady's church is a vibrant, large and fast-growing congregation with many young adult members. He agreed to hold a meeting in his church in March 2003 because of Dr. Jackson's request. Bishop Bady recognized Dr. Jackson as a spiritual father in the city and wanted to honor him.

When we arrived at Bishop Bady's beautiful facility on a Tuesday night, a very gracious, smiling Bishop Bady welcomed us. He was a little concerned about the length of the program since it was a school night. He said, "We want you to come back. If the program runs late, our people will have to leave so they can get their children to bed for school tomorrow." I told him we'd do our best to be out by 9 o'clock, which was an hour past his requested time.

David's presentation was 45 minutes by itself. Not only would we worship, but I had also invited Will Ford III[3] to bring the huge, black kettle that had been passed down from his slave ancestors and to tell the story behind what is now called *the prayer kettle.*

Preparing Hearts for Transformation[4]

Worship is important in every meeting we conduct. Unless the presence of the Lord comes to touch hearts and open hearts, we can have nothing more than a *nice meeting*. We're not into *nice meetings*. We want to see transformed lives. Worship is not just praising the Lord for what He's done, but it's worshipping the Lord for who He is. It's important to focus hearts and minds on the Lord and worship Him face to face. Preparing the atmosphere with genuine, intimate worship is critical.

> Unless the presence of the Lord comes to touch hearts and open hearts, we can have nothing more than a *nice meeting.*

After worship I explained why we were there. "We're not here to watch a presentation, but we're here to participate in what God is doing in the earth. We're here to help answer the last prayer that Jesus prayed in John 17 'that we would be one as He and the Father are one'—and that we would work together in the spirit of unity. Many of you, like me, have not always been involved in unity."

"My grandfather was a member of the Ku Klux Klan. I grew up knowing it, but I didn't really know what it meant." I shared that unlike the Black community where stories of pain are passed down from one generation to the other, it's not true in the White community. My grandfather didn't tell me what he did when he hid behind that white hood. He didn't pass down the details of his shame. I thought the KKK was like a volunteer police department. But instead, it was a lawless mob that took *the law* into its own hands with its brand of *White justice*—from intimidation to terrorist acts of burning homes and lynching innocent people. I don't know if my grandfather lynched anyone, but the KKK did. He aligned with murder whether he himself was personally guilty or not."

Let me pray right now.

> *Dear Father, I come to You in the name of Jesus to repent for my sins and for the sins of my grandfather and other White Christians. I repent for pride, for feelings of superiority. I repent for judging others according to a false sense of righteousness that somehow permitted them to take the law into their own hands. I repent for looking down on Black folk, for passing judgment, for carrying out that judgment and for calling it justice—even lynchings and terrorizing families. Forgive me for racism, for prejudice, and for hatred. Forgive me for insensitivity—for not caring about others' lives. I ask You, Lord, to cleanse me and other White Christians who are praying this prayer of repentance with me. I ask you to break the curse of hatred and racism from the Person of Color who is reading this and from our nation. May instances of overt as well as unconscious racism be covered over by the blood of Jesus. Lord, I ask You to heal every memory of prejudice and racism in the Name of Jesus. I release Your healing power now—to cleanse, to heal and to restore in Jesus' Name.*

The Prayer Kettle

I asked Will Ford III from Fort Worth to bring the kettle that has been in his family for more than 200 years. It had been passed down through the generations from his slave ancestors. "It's like a memorial stone from Joshua 4:5-7. The Lord commanded the children of Israel to look at the stones and remember. The same God who opened the Red Sea—the same God who delivered the children of Israel from Egypt—will deliver you. The Lord knew there was a generation coming behind who would be the recipients of the blessings and the sacrifices from those who had gone before them. This kettle is a memorial stone for me and my family that says, *the same God that broke the power of slavery will fight your battles for you.*"

You Can Agree in Prayer with Generations Gone By

Will told about how the Lord connected him with Dutch Sheets,[5] pastor and leader from Colorado Springs. Will heard Dutch speaking about agreement in prayer—that God wants agreement between the denominations, between the races and between the generations. Dutch shared how God told him to come into agreement with the founder of the Bible school, Christ For the Nations Institute in Dallas, he had attended. Dutch told the Lord he didn't understand that because the founder was dead, and he knew the Lord wasn't into talking to the dead. The Lord answered, "But his prayers are not. They're still alive before My throne. There are some things I want to release into this school but I can't until this generation comes into agreement with that generation. I want the synergy of the ages."

When Will heard that he began to weep because the Lord took him back to the kettle that had been in his family for generations. They had used it for cooking, for washing clothes and for prayer. The masters wanted their slaves to be Christians, and they'd say, "Slaves, be obedient to your masters, if you want to go to heaven." But they didn't want them to pray, *because they figured prayer would foster hope and if they got hope, they would run away.* Wicked masters beat slaves brutally even leading to their death for small infractions. "In spite of his threats and in spite of his cruelty, and because of their love for Jesus, they prayed anyway. They would take this kettle pot into a barn late at night. They'd turn it upside down and prop it up with rocks. They'd lie down on the ground and pray under the kettle so it would muffle their voices as they prayed through the night. The story that was passed down with the kettle was this—that they didn't think they'd see freedom in their time so they prayed for the freedom of their children and the next generations."

> They didn't think they'd see freedom in their time so they prayed for the freedom of their children and the next generations.

Agreeing with Slaves' Prayers

As Will listened to Dutch, he realized he could come into agreement with the prayers his ancestors prayed under the kettle for this next generation. He was reminded of Revelation 5:8 that talks about bowls of incense in heaven filled with the prayers of the saints. That confirmed that the prayers prayed under the kettle are still alive and can be agreed with. "Wouldn't it be just like God to use the prayers of a slave generation to free a nation up for revival again?"

Will made this conclusion, "If my ancestors had been Muslims or Buddhists, I'd have no connection to this kettle's history, but because they were Christians, not only are they my ancestors or forefathers, but they're yours, too—no matter what race you are. I say that because there were a group of White believers back then who knew that any Native Americans or Black Americans who were Christians were their brothers. And they laid down their lives for them. They had their houses burned, were shot and lynched. They were a part of a godly remnant that *prayed in* the First and Second Great Awakenings. God is looking for another godly remnant that will come together in broken-ness, humility and unity and come into agreement for the freedom of the next generation in this nation."

Will prayed in agreement with the prayers of his ancestors: "Lord, You broke the power of slavery in their day. Lord, You broke the power of Dred Scott [the Supreme Court Decision that said that slaves were not persons under the law]. You can break the power of Roe v. Wade and free the womb in this nation. We believe that You can break the power of abortion and break that curse off of our nation. Send an-other Awakening, Lord, that we can finish the business of William Seymour, C. H. Mason, Charles Finney, and other Black and White re-vivalists. Release a mantle of intercession upon us that we might agree in prayer for revival in our day. Reveal Your Son in our nation, God. Will You awaken the church in America to its desperate need of You? And will you awaken the Black church, the White church, and the Red church to its desperate need of each other? We pray that the informa-tion that will be given out tonight will be like a Hilkiah giving the scroll to a Josiah and the history of our forefathers will awaken us to the God of our fathers and their passion for the Living God. Lord, come, come and visit us in Jesus' Name."

I'm detailing this meeting to you because what happened there is foundational to what God wants to do across our nation.

A Prophetic Song

Falma Rufus picked up the microphone and began to sing a prophetic song.

> Awake, O nation, rise up and move. Awake, O My
> people. Come to a crying place where you call My
> name before a broken generation. For in this hour, I'll
> show My power for a brand new day. Awake, awake,
> who will answer the call from heaven? Awake,
> awake out of your slumbering state. Hear the Fa-
> ther's heart saying, "Close every breach from gen-
> eration to generation. And let My glory, let My glory
> come and show you My power. For in this hour, I've
> waited long enough. In this hour, so many souls I'm
> longing just to touch. When you hear My plea, can
> you open your eyes just to see that as in days gone
> by, as in days gone by I'm coming to pass your way.
> It's a new day, and it's a new way, but who's gonna
> wake up and answer this call I have for you?"

Then Falma walked over to face Dr. Jackson and to sing over him, "It hurt you to close the gap. It hurt you to walk in favor and answer the call, but you know not the reward in this hour for my call." It's absolutely true that Dr. Jackson's obedience to the call to connect with White people, especially with White Republicans, cost him a lot—relationships, church members, and reduced offerings for his church. It cost him other things that I won't detail here. Let me just say that the cost was great, but he is courageous and keeps moving forward. Thank God for him!

Falma continued to sing over the congregation, "So I'm saying, 'Come, O come to a broken place.' I'm saying, 'Come. Close every door to a divided race. I'm calling My people to a higher day.' And I say, 'Awake! Arise! Close every door. And walk out in a brand new way!'"

---

1   http://www.wallbuilders.com

2   David Barton, Setting the Record Straight: American History in Black & White, (Aledo, TX: WallBuilder Press, 2004), 22.

3   Will Ford III is co-founder Of Hilkiah Ministries in Fort Worth. He wrote *Created for Influence* and co-authored with Dutch Sheets *History Makers — Your Prayers Have the Power to Heal the Past and Shape the Future*. Will is a graduate of Morehouse College and Emmaus Road Ministry School. He has extensive business background, travels frequently teaching on prayer, unity and revival and works in the financial sector.

4   All of the quotations are from the DVD of that evening called *Liberty and Justice for All* produced by Justice at the Gate, www.justiceatthegate.org. You may order a copy by calling (210) 677-8214.

5   Dutch Sheets leads a local congregation, Freedom Church, in Colorado Springs, http://www.freedomchurchcs.org. He has founded both Dutch Sheets Ministries, http://www.dutchsheets.org, and the United States Alliance for Reformation. He has authored several books including *Intercessory Prayer* and *Roll Away Your Stone*.

Chapter 6

HIDDEN BLACK HISTORY

GOD WAS SETTING THE TABLE FOR DELIVERANCE for His people. Beginning with worship, repentance for racism, the story about the kettle and mantle of intercession that was released through Will's presentation, the powerful prophetic song, and now Dr. Jackson's words were leading to open hearts to receive David Barton's presentation. Dr. Jackson's presence as a spiritual father in Houston and the words he spoke were every bit as important, if not more so, than everything that happened before and after. Falma had sung that it hurt him to stand in the gap, and that's where he was standing at that moment—in the *gap*, the "breach" between Black and White Christians and between Democrats and Republicans.

Dr. Jackson stepped up to the front to speak.

> And I want to thank Susan Weddington because they brought me to Dallas. I was invited to my first Republican Convention. I've been Democrat all my life. But you know what—Alice Patterson called me the day before and asked me if I wanted to come to a prayer meeting at the invitation of this wonderful

99

> Chair Lady, Susan Weddington. And it was my first
> time to lay eyes on her—on a Saturday morning.
> Now you talk about prayer meeting—and on Satur-
> day morning! And this Chair Lady—you know that
> God has made her so famous. Her name is a byword
> to all the people of the Republican Party because she
> believes in prayer. And her sister, Alice Patterson,
> carried that heavy testimony that God impressed on
> her all over the country. She was on KCOH[1] yester-
> day morning telling the same story. Now what's so
> powerful about the prayer meeting was—now we
> got up at 5 something. Now you gotta hear this. And
> when we got there, there were already 4,000 people
> in prayer. I'd never seen it on that order. So now this
> is not just a game. These, my brothers and sisters,
> believe that God can do something with this nation.
> But the man that you want to hear is David Barton to
> see how God has mingled and co-mingled our his-
> tory together.

Dr. Jackson was preparing the Black congregation for a White man's presentation. What he did was extremely important. He wasn't just sharing scripture. He was transferring his favor to David. And the way he did it was amazing!

Dr. Jackson had taught a Sunday school lesson the week before about the man who was paralyzed and the four men God used to bring him to Jesus. Dr. Jackson said,

> Remember this man with the palsy—paraly-
> sis—paralyzed. The Bible says he was *taken with* the

palsies, meaning he wasn't always like that. And he became an *unbeliever* because it took the Messiah so long to come. The man could not go to hear the Christ because he had the palsy, paralysis, para-lyzed—because he was taken with *unbelief*. When you're dealing with *unbelief*, you're talking about the *mind*—the brain. Unbelief simply lets sin and guilt come and it *shapes your thinking*. It'll mess your mind up! It will make you paralyzed. It will give you pa-ralysis. God sent four people to pick this man up and bring him to Christ. I don't care what paralysis you have, if you let Sister Patterson, Susan Weddington, and David Barton—they can always… It's going to be somewhere about the four men. And they'll pick you up and they'll get you to Jesus.

The fourth person that Dr. Jackson didn't mention was himself. He was painting a picture of four men bringing to Jesus the hearers in that beautiful Houston church—to break the paralysis of the mind, to dispel unbelief. Dr. Jackson's personal affirmation was important because the information David has uncovered could be offensive to some. He was telling the people that he, David, Susan, and I were bringing them to Jesus so He could heal the paralysis of the mind. Powerful!

As Dr. Jackson called David up to speak, it was already time to leave. However, Dr. Jackson leaned over, touched Bishop Bady's shoulder and said, "I want you to hear David. Give him just a few minutes. Are you with me, Bishop? Shake my hand so we can have a witness." Bishop Bady smiled and shook Dr. Jackson's hand giving David permission to continue.

David Barton Shares America's Spiritual History

David's presentation is eye-opening and riveting. His rapid-fire delivery relays information about the Founding Fathers that most Americans have never heard. I'm sharing enough of David's presentation for you to understand the powerful impact it has on listeners.[2]

> I want to begin speaking tonight with an overview. The Bible teaches us that *the way a people views their own history affects the way that people behaves.* God uses history to change nations. Remember King Josiah was trying to get people back to God. In the midst of that, they discovered an old scroll and took it to him. He read it and said, "You mean we used to be like *this*?" That led to revival, simply by reading their history."

> The way a people views their own history affects the way that people behaves. God uses history to change nations.

David used that as a foundation for a *providential view of history,* which few people understand. He then began to share some of the spiritual history of America:

> We're told the Declaration of Independence was all about taxation without representation, or economic issues. The Declaration of Independence says there were *27 reasons* why we separated from Great Britain. I wonder how different we'd be as a people if we studied those other 26 and knew what we were founded on.

Desire for Religious Freedom

David owns over 100,000 original documents that predate 1812. David shows a document from 1762 of the charter for the first missionary society in America.

> King George said they couldn't start missionary organizations because Britain had an established [Anglican] church. He vetoed their missionary programs, Bible societies, and Sunday schools. That's why Charles Carroll of Carrollton and Samuel Adams, both signers of the Declaration of Independence, said they got involved in independence because they wanted religious freedom.
>
> This is not taught in the schools. Educators today say that our Founding Fathers were all deists and secularists–not Christians. But they're wrong.
>
> Out of the 56 signers of the Declaration of Independence, 29 of them held seminary degrees. We are able to recognize the most secular signers such as Thomas Jefferson, but know nothing of the others. Rev. Dr. John Witherspoon published fifteen volumes of gospel sermons and is responsible for two American editions of the Bible. Dr. Benjamin Rush, a signer, started Sunday schools and the first Bible society. Francis Hopkinson wrote the first hymnbook, setting the entire book of Psalms to music. Other signers were significant Christian leaders of their day, but we don't learn about them in school. Our religious

history has been deliberately left out of public school textbooks.

David told us that the Constitution never intended "the *separation of church and state*. There is a separation of jurisdictions, but the Founding Fathers never separated their faith from their decisions." Much of our history has been revised.

The Issue of Slavery

Let's take the issue of slavery, because the issue of slavery was a big deal with the Declaration of Independence. Three American colonies—Rhode Island, Connecticut and Pennsylvania—passed anti-slavery laws in 1773-1774. King George said there was slavery in Great Britain and, "If you're going to be a part of the British colonies, you will have slavery." A lot of the Founding Fathers said, "Great. Let's not be a part of the British Empire anymore!" Benjamin Franklin and Dr. Benjamin Rush cited ending slavery as a primary reason to be independent from Great Britain. Did you know that the desire to end slavery is cited twice as often as taxation without representation in the original Declaration of Independence?

> The desire to end slavery is cited twice as often as taxation without representation in the original Declaration of Independence.

John Quincy Adams, the third president as well as a member of the House of Representatives, was known as the "great hellhound of slavery." Benjamin Franklin and Dr. Benjamin Rush started the first abolition society in 1774, two years before the Declaration of Independence. It was an act of civil disobedience defying King George and the pro-slavery policies of Great Britain.

When the colonies did separate from Great Britain, more than half the states ended slavery—states like New York, Connecticut, Rhode Island, Vermont and Massachusetts. Not all of them did, but some of them did.

We used to study different American heroes—heroes of the faith. David shared many more insights that are too many to detail here. He began to transition from America's spiritual history to voting records on key issues and then on to Black history. He shared his view of history, which is like God's view.

Take the story of David. God tells us the whole story—the story of David's failings with Uriah and Bathsheba—as well as his success with Goliath. My view of history is to tell all of it. It doesn't matter if you offend somebody. You tell the whole truth.

Below are just a few statements from David's presentation. Let me warn you that it looks like David could be trying to build a case against Democrats, but he's simply revealing voting records and the facts of history—the good, the bad, and the ugly.

Little-known Facts and Record Votes

Religious Liberty is significant. Remember the law-suit that happened here in Texas to prohibit kids from praying at football games?[3] I've been involved in seven cases before the Supreme Court. My role in that case was to get sponsors from members of Congress for the briefs filed before the court. We needed the Congress to stand up and say, "We want these kids to be able to pray." I got a lot of [Republicans] to sign it, but only one Democrat. Only one Democrat was willing to tell the Supreme Court that our kids ought to be able to pray at football games!

The same thing happened with the Ten Commandments. Twice the House of Representatives passed [a resolution saying it was legal to post] the Ten Commandments [in public schools]. Democrats in the Senate killed both bills. Did you know that 74 percent of the nation wants the Ten Commandments back in the schools? Leahy in the Senate Judiciary Committee and Democrats in the Senate killed it.

The issue of the Boy Scouts. The whole issue was that the Boy Scouts discriminate. They won't let homosexual scout leaders teach our boys! The Democrats in Congress tried to revoke the charter of the Boy Scouts because they won't allow homosexuals to teach young boys.

Free Speech for Churches bill [Houses of Worship Free Speech Restoration Act]—so that as a pastor you can stand in your pulpit and have the same religious liberty as someone speaking outside on the sidewalk. Makes sense to me. Out of 132 co-sponsors on that bill, only 7 are Democrats, 125 are Republicans.

Forgotten Black History

The first African American to speak in the Congress was invited by the Chaplain and a number of Republican members of the House of Representatives. Democrats opposed him.

Did you know that African Americans started every southern Republican Party?

On the Fourteenth Amendment to the Constitution passed in 1866 that guaranteed freedom to everyone, not a single Democrat voted for the Fourteenth Amendment. Ninety-four percent of Republicans voted for it, but not a single Democrat! Of 134 Republicans, 128 voted in favor of it. Of 36 Democrats in the Congress, zero—not one voted for the Fourteenth Amendment to the Constitution.

The first Black Americans to serve in the Congress were elected in 1870 and they were all Republicans. Hiram Rhodes Revels, the first Black senator, took the seat of Jefferson Davis. Of the first 22 Blacks to be elected to Congress, 13 had been slaves! There were three ministers, seven attorneys, two schoolteachers and eight state legislators.

On the Democratic side, the first Black Democrat was not elected until 1935 and that was out of the North. The first Southern [Black] Democrats were elected in 1973—Barbara Jordan of Texas and Andrew Young of Georgia. Democrats didn't elect Blacks until the U.S. Supreme Court ordered the states to redraw the lines so that Blacks could be elected. For over 100 years Republicans have had African Americans be elected but Democrats were still hostile to Blacks being elected during that period of time.

Democrats Oppose Civil Rights

In 1870 the Fifteenth Amendment to the constitution was passed, which guaranteed specific voting rights for Black Americans. The vote went like this: 81 percent of Republicans—142 out of 174 and 0 percent of Democrats. Zero out of 56 [Democrats] voted for voting rights for Blacks."

During Reconstruction, Republicans passed 23 civil rights laws, which fully integrated juries, voting and education in 1866, 1870, 1871, and 1875. Not another civil rights law was passed from 1875 to 1964 because in 1876 Republicans lost control of the Senate. In 1893 the Democrats regained control of Congress and the Presidency under Grover Cleveland. They worked to repeal Fourteenth and Fifteenth Amendments to take away voting and civil rights. In 1896, the Supreme Court, also controlled by Democrats, reaffirmed segregation.

In 1875, the Republican Congress banned all segregation, but in 1882, the Supreme Court struck down that law, and in 1896 reaffirmed their pro-segregation position.

In those days, Democrats opposed African American education. They did not want it at all—especially not *mixed schools*. They were totally against Black and White being educated together.

The Ku Klux Klan was started to oppose Republicans. [They were the terrorist arm of the Democratic Party.4] The reason more Blacks than Whites were lynched by the KKK was that all Blacks were Republicans and were easier to recognize than Whites. Some Whites were Republicans, but most were Democrats in the South. Of the 4,700 lynchings between 1882 and 1964, there were 3,435 Blacks and 1,297 Whites. Democrats [the KKK] burned schools in several areas where Blacks were educated, such as Memphis, Tennessee. A Ku Klux Klan letter sent a picture of a White Yankee woman being whipped for teaching African Americans.

John Roy Lynch, a Black Congressman, explained it this way, "More Colored than White men are persecuted simply because they constitute in larger num-

bers the opposition to the Democratic Party." Black
Congressman Richard Cain said, "The bad blood of
the South comes because the Negroes are Republicans. If they would only cease to be Republicans and
vote the straight-out Democratic ticket, there would
be no trouble."

Even though we were way past Bishop Bady's time limit of 8
o'clock, the people at Harvest Time Church sat riveted to David's presentation. Hearts had been opened through worship, repentance, and
personal stories. Now the facts of history were being received as truth.

More of the Democrats' History

In the 1880s, no less than eleven different tactics were
used to keep Blacks from voting in the Democrat-
controlled South. There were *literacy tests*—20 pages
of obscure legal questions that most lawyers didn't
even know. For instance, "What specific rights do
you have after you've been indicted by a grand jury
that are different from normal rights when you've
been indicted?" There were also *poll taxes* [a monetary price charged to vote, which Whites could af-
ford to pay but Blacks could not], *White only primaries*, and *gerrymandering* to insure only a small number of the Black population in each district could
vote.

The *poll tax* reduced Black voters in Mississippi from
100,000 to 5,000. Florida and Alabama reduced Black

voters by 90 percent. In Mississippi by 1960, only 5 percent of Blacks were registered to vote.

In 1921 Republicans introduced an *anti-lynching bill*, but House Democrats filibustered to defeat it. *Still today, Congress has never passed an anti-lynching bill.* Democrats killed it every time it was introduced, and it has been introduced dozens of times.

Republican President Herbert Hoover got 77 percent of the Black vote. He lost. Blacks started moving to the Democratic Party under Franklin D. Roosevelt. He didn't do anything for civil rights, but he did start moving a lot of money their way. In 1946 Democrat President Harry Truman tried to do something about civil rights, but his own party opposed him in the Senate.

Modern History

After the 1954 U.S. Supreme Court ruling in *Brown v Board of Education of Topeka* mandating desegregation of public schools, Southern Democrats stood in the way.

When little Ruby Bridges wanted to go to public school in Little Rock, Arkansas, remember that? Democrats said, "No way!" Texas Democratic Governor Allen Shivers called out the National Guard to keep Blacks from going to school in Mansfield, Texas. Democrat Governors all over the South said, "No way do we want Blacks in these schools!"

Let this sink in a minute. During the time of the Civil Rights Movement in the 1960s, there was not one Republican Governor or State Legislator in the South. Democrats controlled every Southern state. It was a Democratic governor who called out the dogs and used fire hoses to stop civil rights demonstrators in Selma, Alabama. It was Democratic governors in Georgia, Mississippi, Louisiana and the entire South that opposed desegregation and civil rights legislation.

> Interesting now that we've got this [integrated schools] solved, we've got African Americans and other kids in public schools that are not doing well. They're in failing schools. Democrats are saying, "No way do we want them out of those schools. You stay right there." They oppose educational opportunity—[school choice and vouchers for poor children in failing schools]. You know, they've been wrong on education for 150 years, and they haven't changed that position yet. They're still fighting good educational policies.

Sad but true. Very few Democrats support giving poor children who are in failing and unsafe schools a voucher so they are able to attend the public or private school of their choice. Democrats oppose allowing tax dollars to follow the child, while losing millions when students drop out. Black and Hispanic Democratic legislators vote against school choice even though over 50 percent of Black and Hispanic children are dropping out of schools. They vote against giving inner city children a way out of failing, unsafe schools. Why? Because the Democratic political machine, headed up by teachers unions, opposes school choice. The most costly vote a Democratic legislator will cast is for parental choice in education.

This played out in Texas in 2005 when two Black Democrats voted in favor of school choice for poor inner city children. The teacher unions recruited candidates to run against Democratic Representatives Ron Wilson and Glenn Lewis in their safe Democratic districts. Former teacher and State Board of Education member, Alma Allen, beat Wilson, a 26-year incumbent. The Texas Observer reported, "For decades, Wilson's reign seemed like the only true destiny in the district. Allen should know. In 1998, she ran against Wilson for the same seat and lost badly. During that race, her candidacy generated little buzz and a mere $10,275 in funds. Six years later—running against the same incumbent and on more or less the same platform—Allen's campaign received national attention and more than $150,000 in donations."[5] The difference was that now the teacher unions were energized against Wilson. Wilson and Lewis had committed the fatal vote—a vote to give parents the option to fully educate their children, a vote for school choice.

Democrats Oppose 1964 and 1965 Civil Rights and Voting Rights Acts

One of the most astounding facts that David presents is about the 1964 Civil Rights Act and the 1965 Voting Rights Act. You would think that since Blacks were nearly all Democrats by 1964 that Democrats supported civil rights during modern history. Wrong!

> Democrat President Lyndon B. Johnson [LBJ] tried to
> get the [civil rights] acts through the Senate. He
> couldn't do it even though Democrats controlled
> both the Senate and two-thirds of the House. He
> only needed 269 of the 315 Democratic votes to pass

it. He couldn't get it done. He couldn't even get it through the Senate Judiciary Committee. So LBJ went to the Republicans for help. Republican Senator Everett Dirksen of Illinois came to his aid. In the end, only 63 percent of Democrats voted for the bills—198 of 315 while 79 percent of Republicans voted in favor of them—165 of 209. *Not one Southern Democrat voted for either of the civil rights acts even in the 1960s!* The accusations now are: all those racists that used to be in the Democrat Party have now moved to the Republican Party. Really? Is that true?

In 2002 in Texas, African American Mayor of Dallas, [Democrat] Ron Kirk, ran for U.S. Senate. He lost. The national media said, "Texas is not ready for an African American on the statewide ballot." Did you know that same year there were *three* other African Americans on the same identical ballot, and they all won? They were all Republicans. Michael Williams for Railroad Commission, as well as Justice Dale Wainwright and Chief Justice Wallace Jefferson for the Texas Supreme Court. That makes Texas the first state in the nation to elect three African Americans on a statewide ballot. All three are Republicans. How does a racist party do that? Democrat Ron Kirk was pro-abortion, pro-homosexual rights, pro-wrong on most issues. The three Republicans are pro-life, pro-Bible, and pro-Christ."

1 KCOH 1430 AM, the oldest Black urban radio station in Texas, established in 1953 in the Houston/Galveston area.

2 David Barton has many resources, http://www.wallbuilders.com/. He researches only original documents and is one of the premier historians in America. His presentation is a portion of the transcript of the meeting at Harvest Time Church in Houston on March 11, 2003. The entire evening is on DVD called *Liberty and Justice for All* and is available by calling 210-677-8214, or http://www.justiceatthegate.org. David has produced a professional DVD and written a book with all of the information and more called *Setting the Record Straight — American History in Black and White*. One of David's most popular DVDs is *America's Godly Heritage*. I wholeheartedly recommend all of his resources. I am deeply grateful to David for the use of this material.

3 Doe v Santa Fe Independent School District, Galveston County, Texas, 1999.

4 wiki.answers.com/Q/Was_the_democratic_party_associated_with_the_KKK

5 Felix Gillette, "Cleaning House," *Texas* Observer, March 25, 2004, https://www.texasobserver.org/article.php?aid=1602.

Chapter 7

SYSTEMIC INJUSTICE

DAVID'S PRESENTATION IS LONG AND POWER-PACKED. Bishop Bady wasn't the least bit anxious about the time. He was pumped! Bishop Bady said, "Certainly we were informed tonight. Now you can pray intelligently. You understand what is right. It's been presented before you in Black and White just as plain as it can get."

Then Dr. Jackson went to the front. He wasn't finished yet! He knew he must protect Bishop Bady. Although Bishop Bady was concerned that members of his congregation would leave, only one lady left early, during the presentation about the kettle. After the event, Bishop Bady received nothing but positive feedback!

Dr. Jackson moved with skill and anointing,

> You've got to thank God for this Bishop Pastor. He didn't really know how you would accept this. He didn't know. He was very nervous about it. But he wanted you for one time to know the truth.
>
> Now I want you to meet the person that makes all this work—a woman who's not afraid. Normally when you take a lady like Sister Patterson that told

you her grandfather was a member of the Ku Klux Klan— they kill you for that. They fight you. You take a young man like Dave stand up and tell you the truth—folk assassinate you. You take a lady like Susan. This lady is the Chair Lady of the Texas Republican Party. She wants African Americans to come back and take over their party. She doesn't care if we're Democrats. She says, "We gave birth to this party—why walk away from it?"

Now I'm gonna give this microphone to her, then your Bishop. Susan made the choice that she was going to let the whole state of Texas know that we can be together and do what God bids us to do.

Susan Weddington Shares her Heart

Susan Weddington picked up the microphone.

In the year 2000 we were here for the Republican Convention and quietly with a hand full of people, we prayed. I had just discovered that African American leaders had birthed this party, and I said, "Where are our leaders?" I went to God and said, "I don't know what the breach was, but there was one. I don't know what the wounds were, but Father, I repent. And I ask forgiveness. And I further ask that I be able to forgive African American leaders who walked away from their party. Father, if you will help us find our history, we will bring our history. And if you will help us find our leaders, I will hold the door open and I will invite them in." Where I serve Jesus is in this position. *Why He put me here?* I ask Him every day. I don't know. But I'm here and there is a reason. What we do touches people's lives. This should be the normal way that we operate in the political arena regardless of what party it is. First honoring the Lord Jesus Christ, our Savior, and then opening the door for others to come in. So, come on in! Bishop, thank you and bless you.

The program was packed, and it was longer than I thought it would be! After Susan spoke, it was close to 10 P.M. Dr. Jackson motioned for his worship leader, DuWayne Davis, to come forward and sing "The Lord's Prayer." Everyone was on their feet praising the Lord. The Holy Spirit was in charge. And His presence was heavy upon us. When Bishop Bady picked up the microphone for the last time, he was singing, "Hallelujah, hallelujah, hallelujah." Before the meeting started, Bishop was concerned about getting out on time. Now he was singing praises to God with no regard for time.

Forgive Us for Walking in Ignorance

Hallelujah, hallelujah, hallelujah! Bless Your wonderful, wonderful name, God. Thank you, Lord. Thank you for uniting us, Lord. Thank you for giving us truth. Thank you for opening up ways for us. Hallelujah, hallelujah, oh, yes, Lord.

Then Bishop Bady spoke soberly.

Now Father, forgive us for walking in ignorance. Forgive us, God, for being judgmental. Forgive us for not seeking to know the truth. We have swallowed what was spoon-fed to us with no question. We repent of this, God. Father, Your Word is true. Your people are destroyed for the lack of knowledge. But You send truth to set us free. And we clap our hands tonight because we're free!

Hallelujah, oh bless Your wonderful name. Now Father, for these who have come and given us insight—thank you for Susan. Thank you for Alice. Thank you for David. Thank you for Pastor C. L. Jackson and these other pastors and leaders that are standing here.

Father, you've counted us worthy to hear, and we're grateful. We surrender to You, God. We yield the more to You. Let your anointing touch us even the more. And as we hold hands and lift them up to You, God, we pray that what we experience right now will not end right now, but it will carry us on and on. I'm so glad. Thank You for allowing us to hear this. We're changed eternally.

It was 10:30 P.M. when Bishop Bady closed us in prayer. It was late. You can imagine that members of his congregation rushed out the door. That's not what happened. People stood in line to greet David, Will, Dr. Jackson, Falma, Susan, and me. A mother asked our photographer to take a picture of her little girl with the kettle.

A young adult man from Harvest Time grabbed my hand and thanked me over and over for bringing them the truth. We'll never know how deeply hearts were touched and lives were changed.

We had already seen some of the principles work in other contexts, but the Lord confirmed them again.

PRINCIPLE: The presence of God is essential for personal and national transformation.

PRINCIPLE: When you deal with racial wounds by acknowledging the pain and repenting for racism, hearts are healed and lives are changed.

PRINCIPLE: After welcoming the presence of God and repenting for racism, the whole truth of history can be presented. Without repentance, the pain speaks louder than the information.

In Bishop Bady's words, "Lives were changed eternally," including mine. I had witnessed Black Americans experiencing deep racial healing. They were excited and liberated. This is all I wanted to do. I was involved in lots of prayer initiatives, but what I truly wanted to do was to see Black Americans receive healing and deliverance.

Not long after the event at Harvest Time Church, David, Susan, Dr. Jackson, and I were in Washington, D.C. together for a Justice at the Gate meeting. I thought I knew Dr. Jackson and his background, but a casual conversation proved me wrong and deeply upset me. That conversation uncovered systemic injustice in the political arena.

Shocking Information Revealed

"Dr. J.," I asked, "tell us your experience as a national delegate to the Democrat convention."

"I've never been a delegate."

"You mean you've never been a national delegate. You *have* been a state delegate, haven't you?"

"No, I've never been to a political convention until Miss Susan asked me to pray at the Republican Convention."

"Well, surely you've been to a precinct convention since there's a polling place at your church."

"No. I've never heard of a precinct convention."

I couldn't believe my ears! Dr. Jackson had never participated in his own party's process!! Let me explain in case you're not a political activist. The *ELECTORAL PROCESS*—Primary, General, and Local Elections—is where registered voters select from candidates on the ballot. Dr. Jackson had been very engaged in the electoral process. The *PARTY PROCESS* is where delegates elect party officials who run the party structure of the Democratic or Republican parties. The party or convention process is also where platforms, which describe the parties' values and legislative agenda, are voted on. The two things—electing officers and selecting a platform—are both extremely important. Having a seat at the decision-making table in this process is available to all *who know about it* and participate in the Primary Election. However, Dr. Jackson was telling me that he didn't have a seat at the table in his party. He hadn't been given *access* to the *real power* in his own party—the Democratic Party. Remember that word *access,* and I'll come back to it later.

Because of a conversation I'd had with my friend Cathe years ago, I knew what Dr. Jackson was describing was true of the Democratic Party in Ector County (Odessa, Texas), where I had lived for 30 years. When the Lord began to open my eyes to racism and His desire for reconciliation, Cathe helped me recognize my blind spots. Hold onto your heart here. Whether you're a Person of Color or White, this will not be an easy portion to read.

I knew my grandfather was a racist because somehow I knew that he was a member of the KKK many decades before I was born. However, I didn't remember instances of racism in my own life or that of my immediate family. However, Cathe asked me some questions about things common in the White community in the 1940s and 1950s. This is important for White Christians who don't think they're racist. Cathe asked me, "Did you ever say, 'Eenie meenie minie mo, catch a ------ by the toe? If he hollers let him go.' Or when racing to see who can get to a certain place first to say, 'Last one there is a ------ tar baby?' Or what did you call a Y-shaped piece of a tree limb with a thin strip of a rubber tire in it to shoot rocks?" It wasn't called a slingshot then. We called it a ------ shooter. I was stunned. I was guilty on all counts. Who taught me those things? When I was playing those *games* I was playing mostly with my cousins—with members of my family. If you're less than 40 years old or didn't grow up in the South, you may have escaped some of these racial slurs and pejorative terms. However, I'm sure that many reading these words are shaken to realize that they used racist terms, at least when they were children. Of course, I never said these things *to* a Black person. I wasn't an *overt racist*. I was an *unconscious racist*. I accepted things as they were and didn't ask questions. I didn't question the status quo. *Lord, forgive me.*

While I'm here, let me address a few other things that I bring up before White audiences to help them see our own racism. Have you ever wondered why *flesh* is the name of a color in a box of Crayons that is light beige? What do *flesh-colored* Band-Aids look like on Black or Brown skin? Those are not huge things on the *racism barometer*, but little things matter. Our perceptions of each other matter. What we say and do in private matters.

Before we go any further, let's pray.

> *Dear Father, I ask You to forgive me for the things I said and did in private that disclose prejudice, discrimination, and racism. I and my fathers have sinned. I pray for those who are reading this. For White Christians, Lord, I ask You to cleanse every heart, to further enlighten each person about specific things in their lives that they participated in or condoned by their inaction. For Black Christians, I ask you to forgive me and others who said and did things to you because you're Black. Forgive the actions of children and adults alike. For Hispanics, Asians, Native Americans, Arabs, and every Person of Color—please forgive us for demeaning and dishonoring you. Forgive us for ignoring you. Lord, I ask for Your healing balm to penetrate each mind, the emotions and the will of individuals reading these words. I release God's power to heal memories, to bring down strongholds, and to set you free in Jesus' name. Amen.*

Cathe helped me to see my own racism. Cathe was a Democrat. She had run for city council. She had served on the Board of Directors for Planned Parenthood. She even served as liberal Democrat Ann

Richards' West Texas Coordinator in her successful bid for governor. In addition, Cathe had managed the Democratic phone banks in Ector County for ten years before she had a life change and became pro-life. Cathe was a bona fide Democrat.

I had questioned Cathe about how Democrats dealt with Blacks and Hispanics during election season. "We bought tacos and beer for Hispanics and barbeque for Blacks. Then we bused them all to the polls."

"What did you do about precinct conventions?" I asked.

Cathe was silent for a minute as the realization hit her. "We didn't tell them about precinct conventions." Cathe was surprised at the revelation because she was trying to help me identify my own racism. But what we both realized is that the way Democrats related to Blacks and Hispanics was racist!

Party Process Hidden from
Black Voters

When I learned how Ector County Democrats treated Blacks and Hispanics—mobilizing them with food and transportation for their vote but keeping the party process hidden, I thought it was just an Ector County practice. Now while listening to Dr. Jackson, all the pieces fell into place. Democrats have courted Blacks (and Hispanics) for their vote, and at the same time, withheld information that would make them equal players in the party of their choice—the Democratic Party. Prior to the 2008 election, 91 percent of Black Americans consistently voted for Democrats on the national ticket. However, 96 percent of Blacks supported Barack Obama for president in 2008. Even with a Black American on the ballot, most Blacks did not participate in the *party* process. They were only engaged in the *election* process. Black

Americans, then, are not really Democrats. They're not a part of the Democratic Party process. They just *vote* Democrat.

> Black Americans, then, are not really Democrats. They're not a part of the Democratic Party process. They just vote Democrat.

"You're just splitting hairs," you may be saying. Not so. Stay with me here. Black Americans *believe* they are Democrats. They are the most loyal voting block that Democrats have. But they don't have the power that engaging in the party process brings. They're not at the table. Now back to *access*.

That word *access* is important, especially in the Black community. Several years ago a friend in a large Texas city participated in an initiative to bring understanding between White evangelicals on the north side of town and Black evangelicals on the south side of town. Every month a small group of Black and White pastors and leaders met in a different home to build relationships and try to understand each other. In a conversation my friend said, "Please pray. Next month we're going to discuss politics—why Black evangelicals are Democrats and White evangelicals are Republicans." The report after the meeting was enlightening. She told me that this was the first discussion they had ever had where there was emotion and a little tinge of anger as a famous Black pastor clinched his teeth under the scrutiny from his White friends. The pastor finally blurted, "Access. We're Democrats because of *access*." When I heard the report, it made me sad. The perception from Black evangelicals is that Democrats give them *access* into the political and governmental arena, but just the opposite is true.

Barack Obama's presidential campaign brought many more Black voters in Texas into the party process than ever before. In the winter of 2008 I watched Senator Obama on television speaking from a large convention center in Houston urging everyone to go to their precinct conventions. Never before had the election been so close in the Democratic Primary that attending a precinct convention mattered in the election outcome. Al Gore was the clear nominee in 2000, just as John Kerry was in 2004. But 2008 was different. Barack Obama and Hillary Clinton were in a real horse race! The election could come down to the few delegates chosen in the precinct conventions. (The Republican process is different. No delegates are chosen from the precinct conventions in Texas. They are all chosen on the Primary Election ballot. In the Democratic Primary, the majority of delegates are chosen from the Primary Ballot with a small percentage chosen at the precinct conventions.)

Watching Senator Obama telling the vast audience that it was important to show up at their precinct convention exhilarated me. Finally information was getting out to other Democratic voters besides the White elite that had run the Party for generations. Thousands of Democratic voters from every ethnicity showed up at their precinct convention. I rejoiced that Democratic Blacks and Hispanics were finally being invited into the party process. I know of one precinct in Austin where over 400 people showed up in one Democratic precinct convention on March 4, 2008. That's astounding since less than 10 people generally attend a precinct convention in either party. They were there to show their support for either Barack Obama or Hillary Clinton. Most were unaware of the rest of the process—equally as important—to elect their party representatives and to lay out a platform with their beliefs and policies. They were focused on getting their candidate elected. After they registered their support for a candidate, most left before the party business of electing delegates to the Senatorial District Convention, which was in two weeks.

Now back to my story pre-Obama. After learning that Dr. Jackson had been excluded from his own political party, I was angry. Yes. I was fuming. My hands and voice were shaking.

"That's not right!"

Dr. Jackson was trying to calm me down. "Mrs. Patterson, it's okay."

"No sir, it is not okay. It's not okay that you have faithfully *carried the water* for Democrats. You have mobilized your people. You've used your influence to elect hundreds of Democrats. Oh, yeah, you've been invited to have your picture made with politicians. You were even invited to travel to Nairobi with President Clinton, but you haven't been given a seat at the table of your own party. It's definitely not okay!"

Dr. Jackson had shared just that morning that President Clinton had invited him to travel to Africa with him if he paid his own way— which he did. It was pretty astounding to me that the President would charge to go on a trip with him, but this critical information about Dr. Jackson not ever being a delegate made my blood boil.

Chapter 8

INFLUENCE VS. POWER

NOW IF YOU'RE NOT A POLITICAL ACTIVIST YOURSELF, you may not know how significant this is, so let me explain. It's the difference between *influence* and *power*. Black pastors have always had influence—a lot of it. They open their pulpits to Democratic candidates and office holders to speak to their congregations. They have relationships with candidates and elected officials. They are invited to dinners, receptions, and photo opportunities with elected officials. During campaigns, they are sought out for the votes they represent. However, they hadn't been given information about party conventions, where the political power in their party is exerted.

Most Americans don't know about the process. It's not something taught in public schools. If your party doesn't reach out to you or if someone you know doesn't participate, you probably don't know about it. On the Republican side, Christian conservatives have influenced the Republican Party platform since the 1970s. There was a huge surge in Christian participation during the Pat Robertson presidential campaign in 1988 when videos of what to do in a precinct convention were distributed to potential delegates. That homemade video equipped hundreds of Christians in Texas to go to their precinct convention and secure the votes to get elected as a delegate all the way to the State Convention.

Registered voters who vote in the Primary Election—the election where both political parties choose the nominee who will face the opposite party in November—can participate in the party or convention process. In some states you must register by party to participate in a precinct convention or caucus. Other states like Texas have *open primaries* where you don't register by party and anyone who votes in a Primary Election can participate in that party's precinct convention. Eventually, state delegates chosen from those who participate on the local level elect their officers, including the chairman, vice chairman, and a man and woman from every senatorial district in their state. For instance, Texas has 31 senatorial districts, so 31 men and 31 women for a total of 62 sit on both the State Democratic Executive Committee (SDEC) and the State Republican Executive Committee (SREC). Delegates also vote on their party platform—a set of ideals and proposed legislative agenda for their party. Democrats and Republicans have vastly different philosophies on moral issues, economic issues, and national security issues.

On the abortion issue, the Republican platform has been pro-life since 1976 after the *Roe v. Wade* Supreme Court decision that struck down every pro-life state law in America in 1973. It states in part that "the unborn child has a fundamental individual right to life which cannot be infringed." Democrats' platform has for many years endorsed abortion on demand paid for by you, the taxpayer. Speaking of the 2008 platform, the *Wall Street Journal* reported, "Democrats typically have a strong plank in favor of abortion rights; this year's version is stronger than usual. 'The Democratic Party strongly and unequivocally supports *Roe v. Wade* and a woman's right to choose a safe and legal abortion, regardless of ability to pay, and we oppose any and all efforts to weaken or undermine that right,' it says. Gone is the phrase from the past that abortions should be safe, legal and *rare*."[1]

When I was Field Director of TXCC, I asked the Lord to show me how to reach Hispanics because I perceived them as pro-life and pro-traditional marriage. I wasn't at all thinking about mobilizing Black voters because I equated their values with the stated platform of the Democratic Party.[2] I was wrong.

That afternoon with Dr. Jackson, I began to understand how Black voters could support the Democratic Party even though its stated values were opposite of their own. Now it was clear. The Black community didn't *know* that the Democratic platform supports abortion and the homosexual agenda. They didn't even know there was a platform! Of course, they knew there were conventions, but they didn't know how to participate or what happened in the party process!

Dr. Jackson continued, "They (Democratic candidates and leaders) come into our churches and tell us how bad things are for our race. And if we care about Black folk, we'll vote a straight Democratic ticket."

Moral issues are never discussed. Only race and one-sided economic issues like universal health care are on the table. Black and Hispanic voters are mobilized for the *ELECTION PROCESS* and have no idea

> Black and Hispanic voters are mobilized for the *election process* and have no idea what the two parties or individual candidates believe on moral or religious liberty issues.

what the two parties or individual candidates believe on moral or religious liberty issues.

I spoke with a Black pastor from Chicago who attended the 2008 National Democratic Convention. It was a moving experience for him to see Barack Obama become the Democratic nominee. But it took a Black presidential nominee to open the door for Black participation over 60 years after Blacks started voting Democrat under President Franklin Roosevelt. That same pastor wasn't a national delegate prior to 2008. Why? Because he didn't know about the process!

In my time of discovery about how Black voters had been excluded from their own party process, I was taken aback to learn something else. Cash flows freely to Black pastors and churches to subsidize their efforts for Democrats. Democratic candidates make the rounds to Black churches during campaign season and give *donations* to either the church or the pastor or both to fund their Get Out The Vote (GOTV) projects, to show their appreciation, and in my opinion, to keep them in line.

Electing Barack Obama as President represented a breakthrough nationally for millions of Black folk who never believed they would see a Black President. "Comedian Bill Cosby was so proud to vote for a Black U.S. presidential candidate, he shared the experience with his late mother, father, and brother. The 71-year-old wanted the trio to be present when he cast his vote for the first Black president on November 4, 2008, so he took pictures of his late loved ones with him to the polls. He says, 'I took my mother's and father's pictures from out of a frame, and my brother James, who died when he was six. I put them in my pocket and went to the poll. When it was my turn, I went into the booth, I took out James, Dad and Mom, and we all voted.'"[3]

Bill Cosby's experience and the experience of millions of Black Americans confirm Dr. Jackson's explanation. It was all about race. I could see it clearly, except in one personal instance. In a meeting I attended, a Black pastor friend who had supported Governor Mike Huckabee in the Primary Election reported that he voted for President Obama. I was stunned. This pastor was a Republican. He was pro-life. He couldn't even talk about abortion without weeping, yet he voted for Barack Obama. His actions showed me that the breach between Blacks and Whites in the political arena was much wider and deeper than I could ever imagine. Given a choice between two White candidates, he would have chosen the pro-life one. But given a choice between a Black candidate who supports abortion and a White candidate who opposes abortion, he chose the Black one.

Is it a stretch to say that for many Black voters race trumps values? The actions of my trusted pastor friend confirmed my observation that racial wounds hinder the wounded individual from hearing the truth on any other issue. I wept when I heard the pastor say that he voted for Obama. I wept that his pain was so deep that racism was the most important thing in his life. This is hard for White evangelicals to understand.

Only 4 percent of Black Americans voted for someone other than Barack Obama in November 2008. That's down from 9 percent that generally vote Republican. Black Americans who vote Republican do it for various reasons based upon moral, fiscal, civil rights, or national security issues. However, when given the choice to vote their values or for the first Black president, race and the historic nature of the election were the issues that motivated the vote for over half of Black voters who generally vote Republican.

The year 2008 was a very difficult year. On the strictly racial issue, I am glad that the glass ceiling has been shattered for Black Americans on the national level. Black children now know that nothing can stop them from achieving their highest dreams. I applaud President Obama for this milestone. It's a beautiful thing when individuals rise above race. I just wish the first Black president had embodied the values of the Black community rather than the radical policies of the Democratic Party.

On the race issue, the glass ceiling had already been broken in Texas in 2002 when three Blacks were elected to statewide office. Of course, the national media didn't report it because these elected Blacks were all Republicans.

Michael Williams was elected to the Railroad Commission. Dale Wainwright and Wallace Jefferson were elected to the Texas Supreme Court. Chief Justice Wallace Jefferson is the great grandson of a slave *owned by a judge*. His ancestor was sold on the McLennan County courthouse steps in Waco. Think about it. Now he daily ascends the steps of the Texas Supreme Court to preside over the highest court in the state. The Democratic argument that during the Reagan years all the racists left the Democratic Party and became Republicans just doesn't hold water. Why would a racist party elect three Black Americans to represent their party on the ballot? And how could they be elected statewide when the majority of Texas voters are White? Because God is working in the hearts of men to tear down racial walls and to remove glass ceilings!

That same year former Dallas Mayor Ron Kirk ran as a Democrat for U.S. Senate. Many formerly pro-life, pro-traditional marriage Democrats are forced to change their values to get the Democratic

Party nomination. That was true of Black Mayor Kirk. Ron Kirk reassured a Black friend of mine that he was personally pro-life saying, "I would never cast a vote to destroy an unborn baby." However, his position papers said otherwise. Kirk tried to smooth over his position by stating that "abortions should be safe, legal and rare," but he had to satisfy Democrats by adding, "The decision to terminate a pregnancy is best left between a woman and her doctor."[4] Many pro-life Democrats have changed their position to run on the Democratic ticket, including Rev. Jesse Jackson.

Rev. Jesse Jackson Changes Abortion Stance

In January of 1977, Rev. Jesse Jackson wrote an article for *National Right to Life News* that stated in part, "Those advocates of taking life prior to birth do not call it killing or murder; they call it abortion. They further never talk about aborting a baby because that would imply something human. Rather they talk about aborting the fetus. Fetus sounds less than human and therefore can be justified.... Human life itself is the highest human good, and God is the supreme good because He is the giver of life. That is my philosophy. Everything I do proceeds from that religious and philosophical premise."

However, since then, Jackson has adopted an openly pro-abortion view, believing the right of a woman to terminate a pregnancy is fundamental and should

> "Human life itself is the highest human good, and God is the supreme good because He is the giver of life. That is my philosophy. Everything I do proceeds from that religious and philosophical premise."
>
> —Rev. Jesse Jackson, 1977

not be infringed in any way by the government.[5] While running for president on the Democratic ticket, Rev. Jackson changed his stance. On May 21, 1988, The *Washington Post* published an article by Colman McCarthy called "Jackson's Reversal On Abortion," which stated, Jackson of 1988 says abortion is acceptable because "it is not right to impose private, religious and moral positions on public policy." The 1977 Jackson handily dismissed the privacy argument: "If one accepts the position that life is private, and therefore you have the right to do with it as you please, one must also accept the conclusion of that logic. That was the premise of slavery. You could not protest the existence or treatment of slaves on the plantation because that was private and therefore outside your right to be concerned."[6]

The Democratic argument of formerly-pro-life-turned-pro-abortion candidates for abortions to be safe, legal, and rare is bogus. First of all, there is no such thing as a *safe abortion*. Somebody dies in every procedure. In addition to the death of a baby, a woman suffers. Operation Outcry,[7] a project of The Justice Foundation, has collected over 2,000 affidavits from women who have had abortions. The women detail the physical, emotional and spiritual trauma they experienced. The affidavits prove that *abortion hurts women.* In fact, the U.S. Supreme Court cited The Justice Foundation's Friend of the Court brief in its ruling to uphold the federal ban on the gruesome partial-birth abortion procedure. The brief was filed on behalf of Sandra Cano, who was the *Mary Doe* of *Doe v. Bolton* (the companion case to *Roe v. Wade*), and 180 women hurt by abortion.

"Citing sworn testimony that The Justice Foundation presented, and acknowledging the argument that *abortion hurts women,* the Court recognized that *some women come to regret* their abortions. 'Whether to have an abortion requires a difficult and painful moral decision' and is 'fraught with emotional consequence,' the Court said. The Court also noted that 'severe depression and loss of esteem can follow' an abortion."[8]

Second, the decision to have an abortion rarely includes the woman's doctor. Planned Parenthood and other radical abortion providers oppose measures like *informed consent* that require abortion providers to explain the development of the baby at the time of the abortion. I've heard heart-wrenching testimonies from women who have said they were told the baby was just a blob of tissue.

Women who were doubtful about their decisions tried to ask questions but found out that there is no eye contact or answered questions. Women were hurried into a room to have their baby vacuumed out of their body.

The sound of the suction machine haunts them forever. Many are left barren and remain childless, weighted down with guilt for what they've done. Organizations like Operation Outcry minister to post-abortive women and help them find healing and peace for their broken lives.

Third, more women died from *legal* abortions immediately following the *Roe v. Wade* U.S. Supreme Court decision than from illegal ones. The main cause of death before penicillin was infection. The difference now is that new antibiotics can successfully treat most infections. A study from one of the most prestigious medical centers in the world, Johns Hopkins University, reported: "Occurrence of genital tract infection following elective abortion is a well-known complication." This institution reports rates up to 5.2 percent for first trimester abortions and up to 18.5 percent in mid-trimester.[9] For the local freestanding abortion facility in your community, with far inferior quality of care, the number of such infections will be at least double that of such a reputable medical center.[10] The actual number of abortion-related deaths for women is hard to determine because bleeding or infection is many times listed as the cause of death rather than the abortion that caused the symptoms.

Why do Democrats, especially Black Americans and Hispanics, whose values many times are biblically based, have to change their positions to run on the Democratic ticket? Because the base of the Democratic Party demands it. Who comprises the base of the Democratic Party? The Democratic Party is controlled by the White elite: trial lawyers, labor union members, *pro-choice* (pro-abortion) activists, i.e., National Abortion Rights Action League (NARAL), gay lesbian bisexual transgender activists (GLBT), entertainers, academia, anti-religious liberty proponents under the guise of separation of church and state, anti-war activists, radical environmentalists, feminists and those who believe government programs are the answer to America's problems. The elite make the rules, choose the platform and select the leadership of the Party. As I mentioned previously, Black Democrats are the most loyal voting block of the Democratic Party, but they are not involved in the party process. So they are not a part of the groups I listed above who control the Democratic Party.

> Black Democrats are the most loyal voting block of the Democratic Party, but they are not involved in the party process. So they are not a part of the groups who control the Democratic Party.

In his courageous book, *The War against Hope,* former Secretary of Education Rod Paige, a Black American, exposes two of the most powerful unions in America—the National Education Association (NEA) and the American Federation of Teachers (AFT). "The NEA doesn't donate to and *help* the Democratic Party; the NEA (and the AFT) donates to and *dominates* the Democratic Party."[11]

Before President George W. Bush tapped Dr. Paige as Secretary of Education, he served as Superintendent of Schools for Houston Independent School District. Secretary Paige is a clear, courageous voice in America today. His book exposes the teachers *unions*—not teachers—for their overt political behavior. "Little is known about the full extent of the NEA's political activities, and [Mark] Levin [of Landmark Legal Foundation] has rightly argued that the NEA's 1800 UniServ workers are really political operatives involved in 'developing and/or executing local association political action.' UniServ comprises 'the largest army of campaign workers that any organization has—*more than the staffs of the Republican National Committee and the Democratic National Committee put together.'*"[12]

Teachers unions and the Democratic Party have a stranglehold on education in America. Education is a huge issue in the Black community. A quality education has been denied Black children in our inner cities simply because their parents don't have the resources to choose a Christian or other private school to meet their child's educational needs. Parents are unable to remove their children from violent and harmful influences such as gangs in failing and unsafe public schools. Democratic legislators (Black, White, and Hispanic) vote against the interests of the Black and Hispanic community on parental choice in education, abortion restrictions, and same-sex marriage because the teachers unions give large sums of money to Democratic candidates who oppose school choice.

I've already shared what the teachers unions did to the two Democratic legislators who supported school choice in Texas in 2005.

The Democratic Platform opposes school choice and vouchers for parents to use to give inner city poor children more educational options. During the civil rights struggle of the 1960s, it was Democratic Governors who stood against desegregation in the South. The same Democratic Party that stood at the door of White public schools to stop Black children from entering in the 1950s and 1960s, again in our era stands in the door of public schools to keep poor children inside failing, unsafe schools. Although parental choice in education in the form of vouchers for low-income students would help Black and Hispanic children, Democratic legislators say, "No!" They're blocking the door to educational freedom today just as they did in Little Rock, Arkansas, when "the Little Rock nine" tried to enter Little Rock High School and when little Ruby Bridges walked up the steps of the then-segregated William Frantz Elementary School in New Orleans. Democrats time and time again vote against Black interests but are still supported by Black voters.

Since the eye-opening insight from Dr. Jackson, I've asked the question when I speak before Black pastors, "How many of you have ever been a delegate to a political convention of either party?" Only five ever raised their hand. Three were Republicans, and only one was a Democrat before President Obama and one after. One Democrat was a pastor from Mississippi, who was elected as a delegate to the National Democratic Convention in Chicago in 1968, and the other was a pastor from Chicago who was elected in 2008. Barack Obama, also from Chicago, was a friend of his.

The popular myth that the Republican Party is the party of the rich, and the Democratic Party is the party of the workingman is absolutely false. Rich and middle class are in both parties. In fact, 75 percent of Black Americans are middle class or above. Barack Obama's campaign contributions of $649 million set a record. Are the poor actually *INVOLVED* in the Democratic Party or are they *MANIPULATED* by it? Why are Black and Hispanic Christians voting against their values? I believe it's because of a structure—a diabolical governmental structure that manipulates the two political parties. How did I come to that conclusion?

---

[1] Amy Chozick, "Democrats Seek Unity in Preparing Party Platform," *The Wall Street Journal, Politics,* August 11, 2008,
http://online.wsj.com/article_email/SB121830468013527261-lMyQjAxMDI4M
TA4OTMwMDk0Wj.html.

[2] Our ministry prepared two platform comparison booklets called *Democrats and Republicans In Their Own Words* that show verbatim what the two parties believe on abortion, homosexuality, school prayer, school choice and civil rights.

[3] "Cosby's Emotional Election Experience," November 17, 2008,
http://www.pr-inside.com/entertainment-blog/2008/11/17/cosby-s-emotiona
l-election-experience/.

[4] College of Liberal Arts, The University of Texas at Austin, November 1, 2002,
http://www.laits.utexas.edu/txp_media/html/ig/features/0503_01/voter-gui
des/njdc02.pdf. Search Ron Kirk.

[5] http://en.wikipedia.org/wiki/Jesse_Jackson.

[6] Colman McCarthy, "Jackson's Reversal on Abortion," *The Washington Post,* May 21, 1988,
http://groups.csail.mit.edu/mac/users/rauch/nvp/consistent/mccarthy_jack
son.html.

7   http://www.operationoutcry.org.

8   The Justice Foundation, "The Supreme Court is Listening!" *Operation Outcry*,
    http://64304.netministry.com/images/TheSupremeCourtisListening.pdf.

9   Burkman et al., "Culture and Treatment Results in Endometritis Following Elec-
    tive Abortion," *Amer. Jour. OB/GYN*, vol. 128, no. 5, 1977, 556-559.

10 Dr. and Mrs. J.C. Willke, *Why Can't We Love Them Both*, (Cincinnati, Ohio: Hayes
    Publishing, Company, 1971), *Chapter 21*, "Maternal Deaths and Long Term
    Complications",
    http://www.abortionfacts.com/online_books/love_them_both/why_cant_we_
    love_them_both_21.asp

11 Rod Paige, *The War against Hope* (Nashville, TN: Thomas Nelson, Inc., 2006),
    112.

12 Ibid, 111.

PART II

THE REVELATION

Chapter 9

EVIL STRUCTURES EXPOSED

In 2004 MY HUSBAND JOHN AND I TRAVELED TO LOUISIANA as Texas Co-ordinators to meet with other United States Strategic Prayer Network (USSPN) Coordinators from Mississippi, Oklahoma and Florida. Roger and Charlotte Merschbrock, Coordinators for Louisiana, convened the meeting. Dr. Chuck Pierce, who presided over the USSPN, spoke in a church in Baton Rouge. "Let the Lord show you *Saul Structures* in your life and ministry and how to dismantle them," Chuck admonished. As Chuck described *Saul Structures*, my thoughts raced to politics. *Oh my God, Chuck is describing the Democratic Party!* This was the first time I'd ever considered that an evil structure could be connected to and em-powered by a political party.

Now, don't check out on me here. I'll describe the structure con-nected to the Republican Party later. Separate in your mind any person or group of people. The structure is not about human beings like President Barack Obama or Secretary of State Hillary Clinton, former President Jimmy Carter or your local Democratic official. It's not about the millions of people who *vote* for Democratic candidates. It's an in-visible network of evil comprising an *unholy structure*.

Today, I don't know why it's less offensive to speak of *the devil* than it is to talk about *demons*, but that seems to be the case. Satan is just one fallen angel named Lucifer who agitated one-third of the angels in heaven to rebel against God. He continues to lead a rebellion of angelic beings battling against the Lord and the Body of Christ.

> The great dragon was thrown down, the serpent of
> old who is called the devil and Satan, who deceives
> the whole world; he was thrown down to the earth,
> and his angels were thrown down with him.
> (Revelation 12:9)

One strong fallen angel cannot wreak havoc on an entire nation by himself. He needs a network of wicked forces to restrain the Church and to deceive the masses. Unlike the Holy Spirit, who is everywhere at once and can speak to millions of people simultaneously, the devil can only be in one place at a time. By himself Satan would be totally ineffective, but in cooperation with other powers of darkness he erects structures to deceive and manipulate entire nations. "The god of this world has blinded the minds of the unbelieving, that they might not see..." (2 Corinthians 4:4).

Building a structure begins with strongholds in individuals. Strongholds are located in the mind—the principal place of the enemy's attack. Ed Silvoso, in his book *That None Should Perish*, describes a stronghold as "a mindset impregnated with hopelessness that causes us to accept as unchangeable situations that we know are contrary to the will of God."[1] Strongholds have to do with thoughts, perceptions and belief systems.

"I'll never amount to anything."

"This is a White man's world."

"That's not my place."

"I can't do that—I'm a woman."

George Otis Jr.[2] defines spiritual strongholds as "invisible structures of thought and authority that are erected through the combined agency of demonic influences and human will."[3] Therefore, for a stronghold to take root in your mind, you must cooperate with or at least acquiesce to demonic influences working to deceive, discourage, and limit you. Think about it. Isn't it easier to believe the negative rather than the positive about yourself?

> For a stronghold to take root in your mind, you must cooperate with or at least acquiesce to demonic influences working to deceive, discourage, and limit you.

Some people have healthy and even over-active egos. But for the most part, people are insecure and feel inadequate. At least that's true of me. In fact, a few years ago I was studying information about *motivational gifts* trying to discover my gift from the list in Romans 12:6-8. I found my gift of Exhorter by identifying with the list of *weaknesses* rather than the *strengths*. When you're already down on yourself, it's easy to cooperate with the enemy when he tells you negative things.

You probably agree that strongholds can be in the mind. You may have believed something in your lifetime that you later found to be false. However, when we talk about strongholds leading to structures in a physical location or territory, you may roll your eyes and shrug it off. Stay with me.

Cindy Jacobs describes strongholds as "fortified places Satan builds to exalt himself against the knowledge and plans of God."[4] George Otis Jr. writes, "Peter Wagner and others have pointed out in earlier writings that the Bible touches on the subject of spiritual territoriality in both Testaments.[5] The most cited instance is the prince of Persia in Daniel 10. Here we have a well-defined case of an evil spiritual being ruling over an area with explicitly prescribed boundaries. Even nonscholars must regard it as significant that this creature is not referred to as the prince of China or the prince of Egypt. When this passage is studied in tandem with verses such as Ezekiel 28:12-19 (the king of Tyre)…and Ephesians 6:12 (world rulers), the case for spiritual territoriality becomes even more compelling."[6]

I've experienced spiritually-controlled places where you could feel the influence of evil spirits—you know, it feels creepy. One was in Buenos Aires, Argentina, in the city cemetery near the back wall where writing and graphics revealed that blood sacrifices had taken place. Another was in Las Vegas when I stepped off the plane and walked into the corridors where people were feverishly feeding slot machines lined up against the wall. In both places I was overwhelmed with evil and could feel it on my skin. I just wanted to get out of there.

Another instance happened shorly after we moved into a different house in 1979. I used to be afraid of the dark when I was a child but had been set free from fear long before. However, I found myself afraid when I would get up in the middle of the night. I was frightened—especially in the front bathroom. I would tell myself that being fearful was silly, that there was nothing there, but it still felt eerie.

One night we had the Gibas, a couple from our church, over for dinner. Roger said, "I've been in this house before. A guy from Amoco used to live here. He committed suicide in this house." Bingo!

"I bet I can tell you where it happened," I replied. "In the front bathroom!" After Roger and Peggy left, John and I prayed through our house. We applied the blood of Jesus all over it, especially in the bathroom. We commanded every evil spirit—especially suicide, death, and fear—to get out in the name of Jesus. I was never afraid again.

That's a pretty minor occurrence, but it validates the concept that demonic entities can inhabit a specific location. Those were ground-level demons, not ruling principalities.

A biblical example in Mark 5:1-17 describes the region called the Gadarenes as a friendly locality for demons. A man from the tombs with an *unclean spirit* had been living in a cemetery. "And no one was strong enough to subdue him anymore even with a chain" (Mark 5:3). Jesus asked the demon-possesed man his name. The man replied, "My name is Legion; for we are many." The demons speaking through the man began to beg the Lord not to send them *out of the region*. So Jesus cast the demons into a herd of pigs which ran headlong into the sea. If the demons could no longer possess the man, they would settle for oppressing pigs! The pigs drowned, but the demons stayed in the region. You can't kill a demon. [The same demonic forces that were in Israel during the time Jesus walked the earth are still here. They will eventually be bound for a thousand years (Revelation 20:2) and finally will be cast into the lake of fire (Revelation 20:10).]

After the man was delivered and people came to witness the transformation, "They [the people who lived there] began to entreat Him [Jesus] to depart from their region" (Mark 5:17). The people of the region were more comfortable with the evil forces than they were with Jesus and his miracles. They wanted Jesus, not the demons, to vacate their region. Sadly, many people today are more comfortable with their bondages and deceptions than they are with the truth and the presence of God.

> Sadly, many people today are more comfortable with their bondages and deceptions than they are with the truth and the presence of God.

Strongholds in Government

What about strongholds in government? You won't have to stretch your imagination to consider that the Nazi government in Germany during World War II was under the influence of an evil, territorial structure. It wasn't just Adolph Hitler. Hitler was aided by evil supernatural forces. Myriads of deceiving spirits blinded the eyes of normal people. Hitler's underlings subscribed to his doctrine and carried out the most heinous crimes against Jews and other groups labeled *undesirables* in the Nazi's eyes.

One human or thousands of humans could not have committed the atrocities against the Jewish people without the help of supernatural demon forces. Only Satan and his network of wicked spiritual rulers could have orchestrated such carnage. It took demonic cooperation to deceive an entire nation. That's Satan's expertise—deception.

Wikipedia describes structure as "a fundamental and sometimes intangible notion covering the recognition, observation, nature and stability of patterns and relationships of entities.... A structure defines what a system is made of. It is a configuration of inter-related components. The structure may be a hierarchy (a cascade of one-to-many re-lationships) or a network featuring many-to-many relationships."[7]

Thoughts lead to strongholds. Strongholds lead to structures. And structures make up systems—like systemic poverty, systemic racism, systemic fraud, etc., resulting in hopelessness and generational bondage.

Let me reiterate. It's not people that make up a demonic structure. Paul made it clear in Ephesians 6:12 that "we do not wrestle with flesh and blood [with human beings], but against principalities, against powers, against the rulers of the darkness of this age, against the spiritual hosts [forces] of wickedness in the heavenly [high] places" (NKJV). In his book *The Believer's Guide to Spiritual Warfare*, Tom White describes the hierarchy of Satan's forces in this passage.

> Paul brought light to the topic by depicting the pow-ers as organized in a hierarchy of rulers /
> principalities (*archai*), authorities (*exousia*), power
> (*dunamis*) and spiritual forces of evil (*kosmokratoras*).
> It is reasonable to assume the authority structure
> here is arranged in descending order. Daniel 10:13
> and 20 unveil the identity of the *archai* as high-level
> satanic princes set over nations and regions of the
> earth. The word *exousia* carries a connotation of both
> supernatural and natural government. In the Apos-
> tle's understanding, there were supernatural forces
> that "stood behind" human structures.[8]

Principalities, powers, rulers of darkness and spiritual forces of wickedness describe a demonic hierarchy ruling in high places that *stands behind human structures*. In Cindy Jacobs' book *Possessing the*

Gates of the Enemy, she states, "One of the major strategies of Satan's kingdom is to assign ruling spirits to influence governmental leaders. Once the leaders are conquered, the evil spirits work to get them to enact laws that prohibit any further advance of the Kingdom of God."[9]

At the time I was listening to Chuck Pierce in Louisiana, I hadn't given any thought at all to strongholds in political parties. If I had ever thought about it, of course, it would have made sense, but it was new information. As Chuck's words began to sink in, I asked the Lord, "Father, what is the demonic structure behind the Democratic Party?"

Upon returning home to San Antonio, I received a FedEx package from the leader of the Prayer Force for Youth with a Mission containing a CD by Lou Engle, founder of The Call, speaking to pastors in Colorado Springs that very month. He listed three things God had shown him—three strongholds over the United States of America:

- Kissing the Baal for economic gain.
- The spirit that emasculates men and defeminizes women, which Lou called Jezebel and I later learned was Asherah.
- The spirit of death that demands child sacrifice.

The Lord used the message by Lou Engle to confirm what He was telling me about the Democratic Party. After hearing the CD and continuing to meditate about the unholy structures, I called my friend Connie Fisher in Houston. Connie told me that she had been studying Elijah and was convinced that the structure in the Democratic Party is a *Jezebel structure* and the one in the Republican Party is an *Ahab structure*. She said that Baal and Asherah were both under Jezebel. I agree.

Some people talk about a *Jezebel spirit* meaning attitudes and characteristics of people that are controlling and manipulative. However, for our discussion Jezebel is a historical figure, a human being, a Phoenician princess, who became Queen of Israel by marrying King Ahab. It's important for us to see Jezebel as a governmental figure to understand how a political entity today can give access to the demonic. Queen Jezebel turned Ahab's heart away from God. Ahab "married Jezebel the daughter of Ethbaal king of the Sidonians, and went to serve Baal and worshipped him" (I Kings 16:31).

Notice the time sequence. First Ahab married Jezebel. Then he began to worship false gods. Jezebel was the person with the agenda to worship false gods. Ahab just followed Jezebel's lead.

Ahab had broken one of God's commandments and married a pagan woman. The Lord knew that pagan wives would influence their Israelite husbands to worship their false gods. The admonition against marrying pagan women was not about race. It was about worship.

When Ahab married Jezebel and she became queen, she didn't hesitate to use her husband's governmental authority. Jezebel fed the prophets of Baal and Asherah at her table (I Kings 18:19). Queen Jezebel used Ahab's governmental authority to give access to demonic spirits that became a governmental structure that we will call the Jezebel structure.

Governmental Access to Powers of Darkness

The concept of access is very important—especially in politics. Access gives jurisdiction, a place to stand, and territory. In Ephesians 4:26-27 we are admonished, "Do not let the sun go down upon your wrath, and do not give the devil an opportunity." (The King James Version uses place instead of opportunity.) The Greek word for opportunity is topos, where we get our word topography. The Blue Letter Bible Concordance defines topos as "place, any portion or space marked off, an inhabited place, as a city, village, district, the condition or station held by one in any company or assembly, opportunity, power or occasion for acting."[10] So Paul's admonition is, "Do not give the devil territory, a locality, an opportunity, power or an occasion for acting. Don't give the devil legal jurisdiction by giving him access" (my paraphrase).

When Queen Jezebel fed the prophets of Baal and Asherah she gave a demonic network *territory, opportunity* and a *place* at her table, thereby giving them *national governmental authority*, power, and influence. Before Jezebel empowered the demonic network nationally, they only had power over the people who worshipped them. They were basically a *religious network*. However, when Jezebel used her governmental authority to legitimize the false prophets and their gods, she gave the demonic network an *official governmental structure* to work through.

> When Jezebel used her governmental authority to legitimize the false prophets and their gods, she gave the demonic network an official governmental structure to work through.

many people today are more comfortable with their bondages and deceptions than they are with the truth and the presence of God.

The Jezebel structure was a network of demonic principalities that demanded allegiance, worship, and the shedding of innocent blood. Jezebel's position as queen and her governmental reign legitimized the structure that Satan used in Elijah's day to deceive the nation and lead them into false worship, bondage and God's judgment.

The first principality in the Jezebel Structure is Baal. Baal, which means owner, master, or lord, was the supreme male divinity and fertility god of the Phoenician and Canaanite nations. Jezebel was Phoenician.

The Lord commanded the Israelites in Leviticus 18:21 and 20:2-5 specifically not to "give any of their offspring to offer them to Molech." Jeremiah 32:35 condemns the children of Israel "who built the high places of Baal that are in the valley of Ben-hinnom to cause their sons and their daughters to pass through the fire to Molech." Both Baal and Molech required child sacrifice. For our study, we are using Baal alone. "Modern archaeologists and anthropologists believe that Molech and Baal represent the same pagan god. The wife of Baal is Asherah and the wife of Molech is Ashteroth. Asherah and Ashteroth represent the same fertility goddess.[11] Baal demands child sacrifice in worship. Satan wants to steal the seed, and he craves the shedding of innocent blood.

The second principality in the Jezebel structure is Asherah, the supreme Phoenician female deity and fertility goddess also known as the queen of heaven Astarte, Ishtar, Aphrodite, and Diana.

The worship of Asherah consisted of male and female temple prostitutes. Jezebel legitimized perverted behavior by her welcoming the prophets of Asherah to dine at her table.

False Worship

The Lord told Elijah that He still had 7,000 in Israel "all whose knees have not bowed to Baal and every mouth that has not kissed him" (1 Kings 19:18 NKJV). It's hard for us to understand how all but 7,000 Israelites could turn their back on Jehovah God, the God of Abraham, Isaac, and Jacob—the God who had delivered them from slavery and met all their needs in the wilderness. However, Israelites compartmentalized their lives. Israelites worshipped the One True God as their religious duty, but they also worshipped false gods because they believed Baal and the queen of heaven were responsible for their financial prosperity and protection.

> We will certainly do whatever has gone out of our
> own mouth, to burn incense to the queen of heaven
> [Asherah] and pour out drink offerings to her, as we
> have done, we and our fathers, our kings and our
> princes, in the cities of Judah and in the streets of Je-
> rusalem. For then we had plenty of food, were well-
> off, and saw no trouble. (Jeremiah 44:17, NKJV)

The children of Israel worshipped the queen of heaven, Baal and other false gods because they believed they took care of their basic physical needs.

> The rest of it he makes into a god, his carved image.
> He falls down before it and worships it, prays to it
> and says, "Deliver me, for you are my god!"
> (Isaiah 44:17)

False Gods Demand Worship

The devil and his demons are empowered by worship. Any demonic structure has at its core Satan's strategy to cause people to worship demons. Just as the temptation of Jesus in the wilderness indicates, Satan craves worship. "Again, the devil took Him to a very high mountain, and showed Him all *the kingdoms of the world,* and their glory, and he said to Him, 'All these things will I give You if You fall down and worship me'" (Matthew 4:8-9).

In exchange for worship, Satan offers territory, power, and wealth. He offered Jesus all *the kingdoms of the world*—dominion over nations, governments, commerce, education, and militaries. The offer was real. It wouldn't have been tempting if Satan didn't have those things to give. Satan's offer was a direct assault against the kingdom of God.

Jesus overcame the devil's temptations so that He could complete His work of paying the price for our sins so *we could be His instruments to bring the nations and spheres under Christ's authority.* "The kingdoms of this world are become the kingdoms of our Lord, and of His Christ; and He will reign forever and ever" (Revelation 11:15). The Lord will have dominion over *the kingdoms of this world*—over government, business, education, arts and entertainment, media, religion, and families. But Jesus would not gain the dominion by taking a shortcut and worshipping the devil.

Satan's number one goal is worship. It's the Lord's top priority as well. In the Lord's *top ten*—the Ten Commandments—the first three commandments deal with worship. He commanded that we (1) have no other gods before Him, (2) not make idols, and (3) not worship or serve them (Exodus 20: 1-4). The sin of false worship was so grievous to the Lord that He promised to "visit the iniquity of the fathers on the children, to the third and the fourth generations of those who hate Me" (Exodus 20:5). Those who hate Him are those who worship other gods.

The children of Israel worshipped the God of Abraham, Isaac, and Jacob, but they also worshipped Baal and Asherah so that their physical needs would be met. Stay with me as we see how the same three things: kissing the Baal for economic gain, the shedding of innocent blood and sexual immorality comprise the Jezebel structure hiding behind the Democratic Party today.

1 Ed Silvoso, *That None Should Perish* (Ventura, CA: Regal Books, 1994), 155.

2 George Otis Jr. is the Founder of The Sentinel Group, a Christian research and information agency. He has authored several books including The Twilight Labyrinth, Informed Intercession and God's Trademarks. He is the of the documentaries Transformations, Transformations II: The Glory Spreads, The Quickening and Let the Sea Resound.

3 Roslyn Curry, Health Care and Spiritual Strongholds, Health Care in Christ, http://www.hcic.org.au/archive/Prayer/Health_Care_and_Spiritual_Strongholds.doc, archive.

4 Cindy Jacobs, *Possessing the Gates of the Enemy*, (Tarrytown, NY: Chosen Books Publishing, 1991), 100.

5 C. Peter Wagner, *Warfare Prayer* (Ventura, Ca.: Regal Books, 1992), 87–103.

6 C. Peter Wagner, Breaking Strongholds in Your City – How to Use Spiritual Mapping to Make Your Prayers More Strategic, Effective and Targeted (Ventura, CA: Regal Books, 1993), 35.

7 http://en.wikipedia.org/wiki/Structure.

8 Thomas B. White, *The Believer's Guide to Spiritual Warfare* (Ann Arbor, Mich.: Servant Publications, 1990), 34.

9 Jacobs, 226.

10 Blue Letter Bible Online Concordance Online, http://www.blueletterbible.org/lang/lexicon/lexicon.cfm?Strongs=G5117&t=KJV.

11 Eric Holmberg, "The Massacre of Innocence," http://www.revisionisthistory.org/massacre.html.

Chapter 10

✴

THE JEZEBEL STRUCTURE

THE JEZEBEL STRUCTURE BEHIND THE DEMOCRATIC PARTY began by devaluing the lives of slaves, which is an ideology that devalues human life as a whole. A false theology believed by the Ku Klux Klan (founded by Democrats) and others is called *British Israel*. It's *replacement theology* in which White Christians believe they replace the Jews to become the *true Israel*. All the commandments the Lord gave Israel they believe are given *exclusively* to them. Therefore, the commandment for the children of Israel not to marry pagan women is seen as a commandment against interracial marriage.

The most radical White supremacists today advocate a theology called *Christian Identity*. Their beliefs are so egregious that I will not write them in this book. However, Howard L. Bushart, John R. Craig, and Myra Barnes, Ph.D. wrote a well-researched book that exposes these beliefs in *Soldiers of God—White Supremacists and Their Holy War for America*.[1] John Craig has personally educated me about the activities of White supremacists and their beliefs because I want to know the extent of what Papa, a lifelong Democrat, believed. I would imagine that most White racists do not have a well-formulated ideology like *Christian Identity*. However, men like Papa, as well as many White folk

159

today, believe it's not right to marry outside their race. They don't see it as being racist. They see it as something the Bible teaches against.

As stated before, the first planks in the Democratic Platform supported slavery and the Dred Scott Supreme Court Decision. Once human life has been devalued by supporting slavery, it is easy to devalue human life in the womb.

Democratic Party Platform Opposes Civil Rights

Black Americans, the most loyal Democratic voting block, have suffered the most at the hands of the Democratic Party. The first planks of the Democratic Party platforms in 1840, 1844, and 1846 supported slavery and opposed all efforts by abolitionists.[2]

As David Barton states in his book, *Setting the Record Straight: American History in Black and White*, "For over a century and a half, Democrats have often taken a position that some human life is disposable property—as they did in the Dred Scott decision. In that instance, a Black individual was not a life, it was property; and an individual could do with his property as he wished. Today, Democrats have largely taken that same position on unborn human life—that an unborn human is disposable property to do with as one wishes."[3]

It is tragic how the Black community is unknowingly embracing the genocide of their own race. While Black Americans are less than 12 percent of the population, they have over 35 percent of all abortions. For every 100 live births, there are 53 abortions of Black babies. That's not a surprise if you know the history of Planned Parenthood and its founder, Margaret Sanger (1879—1966). Planned Parenthood is the largest abortion provider in America, and its foundation is eugenics. Sanger was a eugenicist who believed in a superior White race and was an acquaintance of Adolf Hitler, who aligned with her beliefs.

Eugenics

Eugenics is "the study of or belief in the possibility of improving the qualities of the human species or a human population, especially by such means as discouraging reproduction by persons having genetic defects or presumed to have inheritable undesirable traits *(negative eugenics)* or encouraging reproduction by persons presumed to have inheritable desirable traits *(positive eugenics)*.[4]

"*Eugenics* is a social philosophy which advocates the improvement of human hereditary traits through various forms of intervention. Throughout history, eugenics has been regarded by its various advocates as a social responsibility, an altruistic stance of a society, meant to create healthier, stronger and/or more intelligent people, to save resources, and lessen human suffering. Earlier proposed means of achieving these goals focused on selective breeding, while modern ones focus on prenatal testing and screening, genetic counseling, birth control, in vitro fertilization and genetic engineering. Historically, a minority of eugenics advocates have used it as a justification for state-sponsored discrimination, forced sterilization of persons deemed genetically defective and the killing of institutionalized populations. Eugenics was also used to rationalize certain aspects of the Holocaust. The modern field and term were first formulated by Sir Francis Galton in 1883, drawing on the recent work of his cousin Charles Darwin."[5] Charles Darwin, the father of evolution, was a eugenicist as can be seen by the *complete* title of his infamous book, *The Origin of Species of Means of Natural Selection, or the Preservation of Favoured Races in the Struggle for Life.*

Sanger advocated *selective breeding* leading to forced sterilization and eventually abortion because she believed in ethnic cleansing and a superior White race. Respected Black leader Dr. W. E. B. Du Bois, the first Black American to graduate from Harvard, assisted Sanger in marketing her racist strategy in the Black community through the Negro Project in Harlem. Sanger, with the help of Du Bois and other respected Black leaders, under the pretense of relieving Blacks of their adverse conditions, deceived Black pastors into helping wipe out their own people. Over 15 million Black babies have died in their mother's womb since 1973. (If you'd like more information on this subject, you can download *Killer Angel* by George Grant on www.freebooks.com.)

Du Bois wrote about his disdain for Booker T. Washington, who taught blue-collar skills and produced more millionaires from his Tuskegee Institute than Harvard, Yale, and Princeton combined.[6] "Du Bois, in his article *Black Folk and Birth Control*, noted the "inevitable clash of ideals between those Negroes who were striving to improve their economic position and those whose religious faith made the limitation of children a sin." He criticized the "mass of ignorant Negroes" who bred "carelessly and disastrously so that the increase among them...is from that part of the population least intelligent and fit, and least able to rear their children properly."[7] Du Bois was a eugenicist, a part of the Black elite and agreed with Sanger that some Black folk were inferior.

Sanger's radical views were quoted in an essay she wrote in 1929 called *We Must Breed a Race of Thoroughbreds* in which she spoke of a plan for selective breeding that would reduce the need for charities. "It would reduce the birthrate among the diseased, the sickly, the poverty stricken, and anti-social classes of society, elements unable to provide for themselves.... Unable to provide for themselves and their too numerous offspring, they threaten to lower the biological and economic standards of their generation. These classes are now breeding with such uncontrolled fertility that they are a menace to the race."[8] A July 2009 quote from U.S. Supreme Court Justice Ruth Bader Ginsburg shows us that Sanger's mindset still exists in Democratic feminists today, "Yes, the ruling about that surprised me. [*Harris v. McRae*—in 1980 the court upheld the Hyde Amendment, which forbids the use of Medicaid funds for abortions.] Frankly I had thought that at the time *Roe* was decided, there was concern about population growth and *particularly growth in populations that we don't want to have too many of.*"[9]

Planned Parenthood Targets Black/Hispanic Neighborhoods

It's no surprise that the population of Black Americans is declining. Planned Parenthood has built clinics in Black inner-city neighborhoods for years. They are now focusing on Hispanic neighborhoods as well. The abortion clinics are not a sign of compassion but of *intentional, systematic racism* and *genocide.*

The Democratic Platform strongly supports abortion. Most Democratic office holders, like all recent Democratic presidential candidates, are openly pro-abortion. There are very few exceptions in Congress such as Democratic Michigan Congressman Bart Stupak, who led the fight to stop abortion funding in the 2009 health care plan, and a few more exceptions the closer you get to the local level. However, the Democratic platform and most Democratic candidates support government-funded abortion for any reason through all nine months of pregnancy. By placing *the health of the mother* in abortion options, Democrats open abortion choice to any-

> Abortion clinics are not a sign of compassion but of intentional, systematic racism and genocide.

thing that may cause the mother problems, including emotional stress or depression.

As an Illinois State Senator, President Barack Obama was *the only* State Senator to speak against the Born Alive Infant Protection Act, which calls for life-saving treatment if a baby is mistakenly born alive from a botched abortion. Because Senator Obama was unwilling to say that a previable child was a person under the law, he spoke against it and voted present on the bill.[10] Think about it. How many people do you know who would allow a baby to die with no medical treatment if the baby was mistakenly born alive? Not one United States Senator voted against the same bill that passed the United States Senate by a vote of 98-0 with then Senator Hillary Clinton voting in favor of the Act. Some people say that the federal bill was not the same as the state bill, but you can check the facts for yourself here: http://www.jillstanek.com/archives/2008/02/links_to_barack.html. President Obama is truly in a class by himself when it comes to abortion advocacy.

Since the 1973 *Roe v. Wade* Supreme Court decision that struck down every state law against abortion, an estimated 45 to 55 million American babies have been aborted. That is approximately double the population of Texas. Beginning with the post World War II generation, we have destroyed a large segment of our population. In addition to the spiritual and emotional ramifications of abortion, there are financial consequences. At present there are not enough younger generation Americans paying into social security to support the number of Baby Boomers applying for benefits.

The shedding of innocent blood, advocated and supported by the Democratic Party, has given Baal governmental access in America today. The Democratic platform supports abortion for any reason through all nine months of pregnancy paid for by government funds.

Pray with me.

> *Dear Father, forgive us for believing lies. Forgive our part in the shedding of innocent blood. We cry out for your forgiveness on our nation. Lord, we ask You to forgive our President, Justice Ginsburg, and others who are deceived. Give us clean hands and a pure heart so that we may be used by You to dismantle structures in this nation. Open our eyes to see things as they truly are and give us grace to walk in truth, justice, and righteousness. Lord, I ask for special grace for Black folk as they read this book. I pray for discernment, wisdom and courage in Jesus' name. Amen.*

Sexual Perversion

Because feminist and *Gay Lesbian Bisexual Transgender* (GLBT)[11] activists are part of the base of the Democratic Party, it shouldn't surprise us that the Democratic Platform equates special GLBT rights with racial equality.

The 2004 Democratic Platform states:

> We support full inclusion of gay and lesbian families in the life of our nation and seek equal responsibilities, benefits, and protections for these families. In our country, marriage has been defined at the state level for 200 years, and we believe it should continue to be defined there. We repudiate President Bush's

divisive effort to politicize the Constitution by pur-
suing a "Federal Marriage Amendment."[12]

The Washington Blade, the Washington, D.C. GLBT newspaper, reported this about the 2008 Democratic Platform, "The document ap-
parently omits a provision in the 2004 platform that declared the
party's opposition to a constitutional amendment banning same-sex
marriage, which the older document called a divisive effort by President Bush to *politicize the constitution*." It continues. "Leaders of six national gay and transgender advocacy organizations, including the National Stonewall Democrats, nevertheless hailed the 2008 document as
the strongest platform on gay and transgender issues ever approved
by a major U.S. political party. U.S. Rep. Tammy Baldwin (D-Wisc.),
the only openly lesbian member of Congress and member of the 15-
member platform drafting committee, called the platform's provisions
on gay and transgender issues *historic*. Baldwin said the document
would set the tone for expanding the rights of *all GLBT people* in the
next several years. She also noted that the gay and transgender rights
provisions were fully *supported* by Democratic presidential candidate
Sen. Barack Obama,"[13] who is now President.

Will we support a pro-GLBT candidate because of loyalty, tradi-
tion, or party alignment? Are we giving ourselves to Asherah? Realize
that my opposition to the GLBT agenda is not a personal attack against
gays and lesbians who are bound by their sin. We should pray for
them and not against them. I think I adequately covered the concept of
blessing in Chapter Two. Opposing the GLBT agenda does not mean
that we are against individuals.

1 Howard L. Bushart, John R. Craig, Myra Barnes, Ph.D., *Soldiers of God—White Supremacists and their Holy War for America*, (New York, NY: Kensington Publishing Corp, 1998).

2 Democrats & Republicans In Their Own Words – A 124-Year History of Major Civil Rights Efforts Based on a Side-by-Side Comparison of the Early Platforms of the Two Major Political Parties, Justice at the Gate, www.justiceatthegate.org.

3 David Barton, Setting the Record Straight—American History in Black and White, (Aledo, TX: WallBuilder Press, 2004), 24.

4 *Dictionary.com Unabridged*. Random House, Inc. accessed Jun 4. 2010. Dictionary.com http://dictionary.reference.com/browse/eugenics.

5 http://en.wikipedia.org/wiki/Eugenics.

6 Allan C. Brownfield, "Re-examining Booker T. Washington: Black America's Prophetic Leader," The Conservative Curmudgeon, Fitzgerald Griffin Foundation, October 14, 2008, http://www.fgfbooks.com/AllanBrownfeld/Brownfeld081014.html.

7 Tanya L. Green, "The Negro Project: Margaret Sanger's Eugenic Plan for Black Americans," L.E.A.R.N. Northeast, Life Education and Resource Network, http://www.blackgenocide.org/negro06.html.

8 Sanger, Margaret, The Pivot of Civilization in Historical Perspective, edited by Michael W. Perry, 355. "We Must Breed a Race of Thoroughbreds" by Margaret Sanger, 1929, Google Books. http://books.google.com/books?id=NysSmD9t9o4C&pg=PA355&lpg=PA355&dq=we+must+breed+a+race+of+thoroughbreds&source=bl&ots=vqP6Olr7ot&sig=lEbP5quSmDCrqu6NxVyY0dCF7ek&hl=en&ei=3okWS62AG9PVnge907nhBg&sa=X&oi=book_result&ct=result&resnum=6&ved=0CBgQ6AEwBQ#v=onepage&q=we%20must%20breed%20a%20race%20of%20thoroughbreds&f=false.

9 Emily Bazelon, *The New York Times*, "The Place of Women on the Court," July 7, 2009. http://www.nytimes.com/2009/07/12/magazine/12ginsburg-t.html?pagewanted=4.

10 State of Illinois 92nd General Assembly, Regular Session, Senate Transcript, March 30, 2001, http://www.ilga.gov/senate/transcripts/strans92/ST033001.pdf.

[11] Gay Lesbian Bisexual Transgender (GLBT) is the label chosen by gays and lesbians to describe their own movement. I use the term GLBT to describe the entity in America today with an agenda to have "sexual orientation" protected under our nation's civil rights laws.

[12] *The Democratic Platform for America,* (July 10, 2004) http://www.ontheissues.org/Celeb/Democratic_Party_Civil_Rights.htm, 36.

[13] "2008 Democratic platform called 'strongest ever' on gay rights," The Outskirts, August 13, 2008, http://thehostess.wordpress.com/2008/08/13/2008-democratic-platform-called-strongest-ever-on-gay-rights.

Chapter 11

FALSE WORSHIP FOR ECONOMIC INCREASE

DR. JAY SWALLOW,[1] NATIVE AMERICAN ELDER AND APOSTLE, teaches four things defile the land: false worship, broken covenants, sexual perversion, and the shedding of innocent blood. In our Western culture, we can readily see the defilement in sexual perversion, broken covenants, and the shedding of innocent blood, but it's not easy for us to recognize worshipping false gods.

In his book, *Secrets of the Secret Place,* Bob Sorge gives the definition of a false god.

> As I was meditating on Isaiah 44:14-20, the Lord
> gave me a definition of a false god. This definition
> helps me because even though in our westernized
> culture there are very few people who actually wor-
> ship figures of wood or stone, we too have our own
> false gods. In the passage, the Lord describes the
> idolaters as saying to the block of wood, "Deliver
> me, for you are my god!" So a god is defined as this:
> *anything to which we ascribe the power to deliver us.*

> Westerners have their own set of false gods—sources
> to which they turn for deliverance when in times of
> crisis or need: money, health insurance, medical
> treatments / prescriptions, Social Security, retirement
> plans and IRAs, credit cards / consolidation loans,
> drugs / alcohol, etc.[2]

Whom Do We Trust?

Are we kissing the Baal for economic gain? How many political decisions are made because of economic considerations? Sadly, Christians choose candidates and political parties because of promises of health care, social security, higher minimum wage, or higher taxes on the rich, etc., just like unbelievers do. What will put more money in my pocket seems to be the number one criteria.

Many Americans look at the Democratic Party as the party of compassion for the poor. On care for the poor, a huge difference exists in the way the two political parties choose to meet needs. Democrats choose government funding and programs. Republicans choose private giving to churches and other nonprofit organizations dedicated to helping the poor. Some Americans rate Democrats as more compassionate because they see government programs as the vehicle to meet the needs of the poor.

Washington Post columnist George Will published an article on March 27, 2008 with facts reported from an article that Texas Supreme Court Justice Don Willett wrote in the *Texas Review of Law & Politics* in which he reviewed *Who Really Cares: The Surprising Truth About Compassionate Conservatism* by Arthur C. Brooks, a professor at Syracuse University. The myth that liberal Democrats are more compassionate toward the needs of the poor doesn't hold up when compared to the amazing facts below taken from Willett's article.

- Although liberal families' incomes average 6 percent higher than those of conservative families, conservative-headed households give, on average, 30 percent more to charity than the average liberal-headed household ($1,600 per year vs. $1,227).

- Conservatives also donate more time as well as donating more blood.

- During the 2004 Presidential Election, residents of the states that voted for Democrat John Kerry contributed smaller percentages of their incomes to charity than did residents of states that voted for Republican George Bush.

- Bush carried 24 of the 25 states where charitable giving was above average.

- In the 10 *reddest* most Republican states in which Bush won more than 60 percent majorities, the average percentage of personal income donated to charity was 3.5 percent. Residents of the *bluest* states, which gave Bush less than 40 percent, donated just 1.9 percent.

- People who **reject** the Democratic idea *that government has a responsibility to reduce income inequality* donate an average of *four times more* than people who **accept** that proposition.

Brooks demonstrates a correlation between charitable behavior and *the values that lie beneath* liberal and conservative labels. Two influences on charitable behavior are *religion* and *attitudes about the proper role of government.*

Willet found that the most important gauge of an individual's generosity is *religion*. "It increasingly correlates with conservative po-

> Two influences on charitable behavior are religion and attitudes about the proper role of government.

litical affiliations because, as Brooks' book says, 'the percentage of self-described Democrats who say they have 'no religion' has more than quadrupled since the early 1970s.' America is largely divided between religious givers and secular non-givers, and [religious givers] are disproportionately conservative."

The Chronicle of Philanthropy ranks Austin, Texas, as 48th out of America's 50 largest cities in per capita charitable giving. Austin is Texas' most liberal city. Travis County, where Austin is, was the only county of the 254 Texas counties that opposed the 2005 Marriage Amendment that stated marriage in Texas is between one man and one woman. The other 253 counties in Texas supported the Marriage Amendment, some by 94 percent. In 2004, Austin also voted 56 percent for Democratic Candidate John Kerry while he garnered only 38 percent statewide. "Brooks' data about disparities between liberals' and conservatives' charitable giving fit these facts: Democrats represent a majority of the wealthiest congressional districts, and half of America's richest households live in states where *both* senators are Democrats." Although Austin rates near the bottom in charitable giving, you wouldn't know it by the bumper stickers that Justice Willet has noted in Austin—*Better a Bleeding Heart Than None at All, The Road to Hell Is Paved With Republicans, Republicans Are People Too—Mean, Selfish, Greedy People* and *The Moral High Ground is Built on Compassion.*[3]

The biggest difference in the generosity of Republicans and Democrats is that Republicans give their own money, and Democrats give your tax money by way of government funding. For instance, in 2000, Democratic "Vice President Al Gore gave only 0.2 percent of his family income, one-seventh of the average for donating households. But Gore 'gave at the office.' By using public office to give other peoples' money to government programs, he was being charitable, as liberals increasingly and conveniently understand that word."[4]

Black Americans Damaged by Government Programs

The people group in America that has been most damaged by government programs is the Black community. In *Scam—How the Black Leadership Exploits Black America*, Black author Jesse Lee Petersen writes, "The primary tool that has led to the destruction of the Black family and the discarding of the Black man as its head is a program once called 'Aid to Families with Dependent Children' (AFDC). This program was started under [Democratic President] Franklin Roosevelt's New Deal to provide aid to widows with children. The program was eventually expanded in later administrations to include unmarried parents with children. Beginning in 1965 as part of [Democratic President Lyndon] Johnson's so-called War on Poverty, liberals [Democrats] created the food stamp program, which quickly ballooned from 424,000 clients to 2.2 million. This program, added to the AFDC welfare checks, helped create a climate that strongly discouraged Black men from remaining in a family structure. It also encouraged single moms to stay on welfare indefinitely....The welfare system allowed men to impregnate women without guilt or commitment to them or their children. These men knew these women would be getting their regular welfare checks; with no costs to either sex, it served as an incentive for irresponsibility....Welfare robs women and men of self-esteem and self worth."[5] In 1997 under a Republican Congress AFDC was changed to Temporary Assistance for Needy Families (TANF) and opened assistance to married couples, but the trend of single mothers receiving government funding for having children had been solidified for almost 40 years.

Where Is Our Focus?

Back to the central question—who do we depend upon, trust, and worship to meet our needs? Dr. Alveda King, niece of Dr. Martin Luther King, Jr., stated in *A Covenant with Life: Reclaiming MLK's Legacy,* "As a Christian civil rights activist, I can remember a time in America when Black people looked to God for answers."[6]

I've heard Dr. Jackson say that *the focus of many Black slaves was the Lord.* They trusted Him in the midst of treachery, oppression and unjust treatment. Rev. Wayne Perryman in his book, *Unfounded Loyalty—An In-depth Look into the Blind Love Affair between Blacks and Democrats,* talks about how important faith in God is to Black Americans.

> Over the years, our faith in God influenced every-
> thing we did. When White doctors refused to treat
> us, while the criminal justice system mistreated us,
> we called on God, activated our faith, and docu-
> mented our experiences in song, singing, *"He [God] is
> our doctor in the sickroom and a lawyer in the court-
> room."* "Faith" was merely a word in the Bible to
> most people, but to the African American, it was the
> basis for their survival.[7]

Who do we trust today? There is still racism today. No one could deny that. The question is—where is our focus? On government or on God?

World Net Daily penned a verse modeled after Psalm 23. They showed it as a joke, but it is far from being funny.

> Psalm 2009
>
> The politician is my shepherd—I am in want:
> He maketh me to lie down on park benches.
> He leadeth me beside the still factories.
> He disturbeth my soul.
> He leadeth me in the path of destruction for the
> [Democratic] party's sake.
> Yea, though I walk through the Valley of the Shadow
> of Depression,
> I anticipate no recovery, for he is with me.
> He prepareth a reduction in my salary. In the pres-
> ence of mine enemies,
> He anointeth my small income with taxes: my ex-
> penses runneth over.
> Surely unemployment and poverty shall follow me
> all the days of my life.
> And I shall dwell in [government housing] forever.[8]

Democrats Advocate Big Government

Government programs installed when Democratic-controlled Congresses aligned with Democratic Presidents Franklin D. Roosevelt and Lyndon Johnson have become a hard slave master. The current Democratic Congress aligned with Democratic President Barack

Obama is operating with the same unfettered authority. Living on government programs has trapped poor Black and Hispanic folk in generational poverty. It has also resulted in *blind loyalty* to the Democratic Party and its promise to meet all of the needs of the faithful.

Rev. Perryman documents that prior to the death of Dr. King in 1968, 52 percent of Black children lived in two-parent households until they reached age seventeen. Then more Black men were the heads of households, but by 2003 over 55 percent of Black households were headed by single women.[9]

Many Christians obviously don't equate trusting government or man with false worship, but it is.

> Thus says the Lord, "Cursed is the man who trusts in mankind and makes flesh his strength, and whose heart turns away from the Lord. For he will be like a bush in the desert and will not see when prosperity comes, but will live in stony wastes in the wilderness, a land of salt without inhabitant. Blessed is the man who trusts in the Lord and whose trust is the Lord. For he will be like a tree planted by the water, that extends its roots by a stream and will not fear when the heat comes; but its leaves will be green, and it will not be anxious in a year of drought nor cease to yield fruit." (Jeremiah 17:5-8)

No matter our race, are we innocently bowing down and worshipping the god of government? Do we see the demonic powers behind the offer of meeting needs in exchange for total dependence? What is our worship and loyalty costing future generations?

After 60 years of programs designed by Democrats under Franklin Roosevelt and Lyndon Johnson, *more* not *less* people are on government assistance. Instead of empowering the poor, Democratic answers have enslaved them resulting in *systemic* poverty, bondage and hopelessness. That's Satan's goal—"to kill, steal and destroy" (John 10:10).

> "We have substituted government for God. If we'll trust the Lord, He'll give us more than 40 acres and a mule."
> —Dr. C.L. Jackson

Substituting Government for God

Dr. C. L. Jackson said it best. "We *have substituted government for God. If* we'll trust the Lord, He'll give us more than 40 acres and a mule. He owns all the cattle on a thousand hills, and I want one of those hills." Dr. Jackson speaks from years of experience in the pulpit. He has witnessed firsthand the way governmental structures and systems have decimated generations of his people.

> "Has a nation changed its gods, which are not gods?
> But My people have changed their glory for what
> does not profit. Be astonished, O heavens, at this,
> and be horribly afraid—be very desolate," says the
> Lord. "For My people have committed two evils;
> they have forsaken Me the fountain of living waters,
> and hewn themselves cisterns—broken cisterns that
> can hold no water." (Jeremiah 2:11-13)

At best, government programs are broken cisterns that leak vitality and result in dependence on man rather than God. Compared to abortion and same-sex marriage, most of us consider the sin of trusting government instead of God as a minor sin, but is it really?

Dr. Alveda King Speaks

Before we leave the topic of the economy and the Democrats' record on poverty and meeting the needs of its most loyal base—Black Americans, let's revisit the Democrats' record on civil rights in the words of Dr. Alveda King, from her article, *A Covenant With Life: Reclaiming MLK's Legacy.*

> A brief history lesson can reveal how we [Black Americans] got to a place of looking to man instead of God for answers.
>
> In 1960, Senator John F. Kennedy defeated sitting Vice President Richard Nixon in the bid to become president. The Black vote swung the tide!
>
> My grandfather, Dr. Martin Luther King, Sr., or 'Daddy King,' was a Republican and father of Dr. Martin Luther King, Jr. who was a Republican.
>
> Daddy King influenced a reported 100,000 Black voters to cast previously Republican votes for Senator Kennedy even though Kennedy had voted against the 1957 Civil Rights Law. Mrs. King had appealed to Kennedy and Nixon to help her husband, and Nixon who had voted for the 1957 Civil Rights Law did not. At the urging of his advisors, Kennedy made a politically calculated phone call to Mrs. King, who was pregnant at the time, bringing the attention of the nation to Dr. King's plight.

Moved by Mrs. King's gratitude for Senator Kennedy's intervention, Daddy King was very grateful to Senator Kennedy for his assistance in rescuing Dr. King, Jr. from a life-threatening jail encounter. This experience led to a Black exodus from the Republican Party.

Thus, this one simple act of gratitude caused Black America to quickly forget that the Republican Party was birthed in America as the antislavery party to end the scourge of slavery and combat the terror of racism and segregation. They quickly forgot that the Democratic Party was the party of the Ku Klux Klan.

Banished from memory was the fact that the Democratic Party fought to keep Blacks in slavery and in 1894 overturned the civil rights laws of the 1860s that had been passed by Republicans, after the Republicans also amended the Constitution to grant Blacks freedom, citizenship and the right to vote.

Forgotten was the fact that it was the Republicans who started the HBCUs (Historically Black Colleges and Universities) and the NAACP (National Association for the Advancement of Colored People) to stop the Democrats from lynching Blacks. Into the dust bin of history was tossed the fact that it was the Republicans led by Republican Senator Everett Dirksen who pushed to pass the civil rights laws in 1957, 1960, 1964, 1965 and 1968.

Removed from memory are the facts that it was Republican President Dwight Eisenhower who sent troops to Arkansas to desegregate schools, established the Civil Rights Commission in 1958, and appointed Chief Justice Earl Warren to the U.S. Supreme Court, which resulted in the 1954 *Brown v. Board of Education* decision ending school segregation.

Meanwhile Democrats in Congress were still fighting to prevent the passage of new civil rights laws that would overturn those discriminatory Black Codes and Jim Crow laws that had been enacted by Democrats in the South. There would have been no law for President Lyndon Johnson to sign in 1964 had it not been for the Republicans breaking the Democrats' filibuster of the law and pushing to have that landmark legislation enacted. It's amazing how Democrats today try to rewrite history before the public. Senate Majority Leader Harry Reid accused Republicans who were opposing the radical pork-filled health care bill to racists who filibustered the civil rights bills. "When this body was on the verge of guaranteeing equal civil rights to everyone regardless of the color of their skin, some senators resorted to the same filibuster threats that we hear today."[10] The problem is that those senators who opposed civil rights were Democrats. Reid knew that he could imply that Republicans were racists and many Americans would believe him. "Historians also faulted Mr. Reid's curious reference to the Senate civil rights debates of the 1960s. After all, it was Southern Democrats who mounted an 83-day filibuster of the 1964 Civil Rights Bill. The final vote to cut off debate saw 29 Senators in opposition, 80% of them Democrats. Among those voting to block the civil rights bill was West Virginia Senator Robert Byrd, who personally filibustered the bill for 14 hours. The next year he also opposed the Voting Rights Act of 1965. Mr. Byrd still sits in the Senate, and indeed preceded Mr. Reid as his party's majority leader until he stepped down from that role in 1989."[11]

No one batted an eye when President Kennedy opposed the 1963 March on Washington by Dr. King. Hardly a ripple of protest was uttered when President Kennedy, through his brother Attorney General Robert Kennedy, had Dr. King wiretapped and investigated on suspicion of being a Communist.

Little attention was paid to the fact that it was a Democrat, Public Safety Commissioner Eugene "Bull" Conner, who in 1963 turned dogs and fire hoses on Dr. King and other civil rights protestors. No one noted that it was a Democrat, Georgia Governor Lester Maddox, who waved ax handles to stop Blacks from patronizing his restaurant. Nor was heed paid to the fact that it was a Democrat, Ala-

bama Governor George Wallace, who stood in front
of the Alabama schoolhouse in 1963 and thundered:
"Segregation now, segregation tomorrow, segregation forever." None of those racist Democrats became
Republicans.

During this time of turmoil, completely forgotten
was the fact that it was Democrat Arkansas Governor Orville Faubus, who in 1954 had blocked desegregation of a Little Rock public school. To their eternal shame, the chief opponents of the landmark 1964
Civil Rights Act were Democrat Senators Sam Ervin,
Albert Gore, Sr. and Robert Byrd, a former Klansman
[and a sitting Democratic United States Senator to-
day]. All of the racist Democrats that Dr. King was
fighting remained Democrats until the day they died.
How can anyone today think that Dr. King, my uncle, would have joined the party of the KKK?

There is a law of unexpected outcomes. Who could
have predicted that the Black exodus from the Republican Party to the Democratic Party in the 1960's
would have also ushered in decades of destruction
which continue to plague our communities today? [12]

Dr. Alveda C. King's article is reprinted in its entirety under Appendix A at the end of this book. Every word of it is full of riveting
truth.

We Christians don't worship false gods intentionally. We've been
deceived. We've believed things that are not true, and we've trusted in
man and in government.

God is a jealous God. He desires our worship, our trust and our service. Pray with me.

> *Father, I open my heart to You and to You alone. Forgive me, Lord, for the times I've put my trust in man and in government. Forgive me for looking to another to meet my needs and the needs of others in our nation. You are our Provider. You are my inheritance, my portion and my deliverer. I put my trust in You and You alone—in Jesus' name. Amen.*

---

1   Dr. Jay Swallow co-founded Two Rivers Native American Training Center. He is the chairman of the Native American Apostolic Council and serves over 300 Native American tribes in the United States, Canada and Mexico. Dr. Swallow has received his honorary doctorate degree from Jacksonville Theological Seminary, Jacksonville, FL. Dr. Swallow is a direct descendant of Chief Black Kettle, Peace Chief of the Cheyenne Nation.

2   Sorge, Bob, *Secrets of the Secret Place*, (Greenwood, MO: Oasis House, 2001), 35.

3   Will, George, "Conservatives More Liberal Givers," *Washington Post*, March 27, 2008.
    http://www.realclearpolitics.com/articles/2008/03/conservatives_more_liberal_giv.html.

4   Ibid.

5   Petersen, Jesse Lee, *Scam—How the Black Leadership Exploits Black America*, (Nashville, Tenn.: WND Books, 2003), 155-156.

6   King, Dr. Alveda, "A Covenant with Life: Reclaiming MLK's Legacy," *The Black Republican*, Fall/Winter 2008, www.nbra.info.

7   Wayne Perryman, Unfounded Loyalty—An In-depth Look into the Blind Love Affair between Blacks and Democrats, (Seattle, WA: Hara Publishing Group, 2003), 16.

8   "Psalm 2009—The Politician is my Shepherd," *WorldNetDaily*, March 16, 2009, http://www.wnd.com/index.php?fa=PAGE.view&pageId=92021.

9   Perryman, *Unfounded Loyalty*, 20.

10 "Reid Compares Opponents of Health Care Reform to Supporters of Slavery,"
    Fox News, December 7, 2009,
    http://www.foxnews.com/politics/2009/12/07/reid-compares-health-care-ref
    orm-foes-slavery-supporters.

11 John Fund, "Harry Reid's History Lesson," *The Wall Street Journal Online*, De-
    cember 8, 2009,
    http://online.wsj.com/article/SB10001424052748703558004574583980985617954.html.

12 King, *A Covenant With Life: Reclaiming MLK's Legacy.*

Chapter 12

⚜

THE AHAB STRUCTURE

WHY WOULD THE MOST PRO-LIFE, PRO-TRADITIONAL MARRIAGE, pro-religious liberty people group—Black Americans—support the Democratic Party, which is pro-abortion and pro-same-sex marriage, as well as its foundation being pro-slavery and anti-civil rights?

Need for Racial Healing

Dr. Alveda King explained how history has been revised and we've bought into the revision. Dr. King also gave amazing insight when she answered the question, "Why did people vote for Barack Obama?" on a YouTube commentary. She said prior to the election, "African Americans will not listen to the pro-life and pro-traditional marriage and family voices because many African Americans have suffered so much from slavery, segregation, genocide and eugenics."[1] The Lord showed her Exodus 6:9 in explanation.

> So Moses told the people of Israel what the LORD
> had said, but they refused to listen anymore. They
> had become too discouraged by the brutality of their
> slavery. (Exodus 6:9, NLT)

185

Dr. King confirmed what the Lord showed me. When racism has not been repented for, the pain speaks louder than the information. For racism to be quieted in a wounded person's life there must be acknowledgment and repentance for racism, segregation, genocide, and eugenics. Only racial healing can quiet the pain to be able to hear new information.

Biblical Worldview

The second reason is true of most Christians today. As a whole, the Body of Christ does not have a *biblical worldview.* A worldview is "a set of presuppositions (assumptions which may be true, partially true or entirely false) which we hold (consciously or subconsciously, consistently or inconsistently) about the basic make-up of our world."[2] A *biblical worldview* is based upon the teachings in the Word of God.

Have you ever entertained the thought that the Bible speaks to almost every circumstance in life—including fiscal governmental issues? For instance, the Lord doesn't take from the rich and give to the poor. In the instance of the ten talents, the Lord took from the one who buried his talent because he was afraid of the master. Jesus told the story. The master said,

> "Therefore take away the talent from him, and give it
> to the one who has the ten talents." For to everyone
> who has shall more be given, and he shall have an
> abundance; but from the one who does not have,
> even what he does have shall be taken away.
> (Matthew 25:28-29)

Don't ask me to explain God's economy. I'm just quoting scripture. It's also interesting to consider the tithe. It would be reasonable for us to think that the Lord could require at least 15 percent from the rich rather than 10 percent from both the rich and the poor. But He doesn't. He asks the same. Of course, we are encouraged to give alms and special offerings. But at no time in scripture does the Lord require a higher percentage from the rich than He does from the poor. It's been my experience that Christians who make a modest income actually give a higher percentage to the church and nonprofit organizations than do most wealthy individuals. Of course, the amount that the rich give is more, but the percentage many times is not.

> It would be reasonable for us to think that the Lord could require at least 15 percent from the rich rather than 10 percent from both the rich and the poor. But He doesn't. He asks the same.

One more point before we leave the *worldview* issue. Did you know that the minimum wage is against the Word of God? Think about the parable of the laborers in the vineyard in Matthew 20:1-16. The landowner paid the laborers he hired early in the morning a denarius. Laborers were hired at the third, sixth, ninth, and eleventh hour. When the laborers were all paid the same wages, the ones who had worked longer thought they were treated unfairly. The landowner told the laborers that they didn't have a legitimate complaint because he had given each one what he promised them.

> Is it not lawful for me to do what I wish with what is my own? Or is your eye envious because I am generous? (Matthew 20:15)

It's popular to think that the government should be able to take more from the rich because it's not fair for the rich to have so much money. But God is not *Robin Hood* (a folk hero who took from the rich and gave to the poor). We must look to the Word of God for direction, even when it comes to government policies.

Limits to the Church's Benevolence

Although the Church is admonished to give to the poor, there were limits to that generosity. What about single mothers? Does the Bible speak to them? Yes. Read the following verses carefully, focusing on current government funding for unmarried mothers. The Bible calls them widows, and the Church is admonished to care for widows who are *widows indeed*. The verses below give parameters for those to be cared for by believers.

> Honor widows who are widows indeed; but if any
> widow has children or grandchildren, let them first
> learn to practice piety in regard to their own family
> *and to make some return to their parents*; for this is ac-
> ceptable in the sight of God. Now she who is a
> widow indeed and who has been left alone, has fixed
> her hope on God and continues in entreaties and
> prayers night and day. But she who gives herself to
> wanton pleasure is dead even while she lives....*But if
> anyone does not provide for his own, and especially for
> those of his household, he has denied the faith and is worse
> than an unbeliever.* Let a widow be put on the list only
> if *she is not less than sixty years old*, having been the
> wife of one man, having a reputation for good
> works; and if she has brought up children, if she has

shown hospitality to strangers, if she has washed the saints' feet, if she has assisted those in distress, and if she has devoted herself to every good work. But refuse to put younger widows on the list, for when they feel sensual desires in disregard of Christ, they want to get married, thus incurring condemnation, because they have set aside their previous pledge. At the same time they also learn to be idle, as they go around from house to house; and not merely idle, but also gossips and busybodies, talking about things not proper to mention. Therefore, I want younger widows to get married, bear children, keep house, and give the enemy no occasion for reproach; for some have already turned aside to follow Satan. If any woman who is a believer has dependent widows, let her assist them, and let not the church be burdened, so that it may assist those who are widows indeed. (1 Timothy 5:3-16, emphasis added)

The Church is not to provide for widows less than 60 years old. If the widow is 60 or older and has not been active in the Church, she is not to be cared for by the Church. If she is younger than 60, this scripture says that she should return to the home of her parents with the object of getting married.

Caring for the young widow (or single mother) is the responsibility of her family. It is certainly not the responsibility of government. Scripture says that if the family member does not care for his own household, he is "worse than an infidel."

Deception

The third reason is a spiritual one—it's believing something that isn't true—it's deception. Deception is Satan's primary weapon.

In Revelation 2, the Lord shows that Jezebel, now a Spirit or territorial principality, deceives and intimidates to gain control using fear tactics and manipulation. Jezebel is the deceiver and manipulator, but notice where God places the blame.

> "Nevertheless I have a few things against you, *because you allow* that woman Jezebel, who calls herself a prophetess to *teach* and *seduce* My servants to commit sexual immorality and eat things sacrificed to idols. And I gave her time to repent of her sexual immorality, and she did not repent. Indeed I will cast her into a sickbed, and those who commit adultery with her into great tribulation, unless they repent of their deeds. And I will kill her children with death..." (Revelation 2:20–23)

Jezebel teaches and seduces.

- *To teach*—"to accustom to some action or attitude—to seek to make known and accepted"[3]
- *To seduce*—"to persuade to disobedience or disloyalty".

Jezebel teaches and seduces through *deception*—"misleads, beguiles, and imposes false ideas that cause confusion and helplessness to further the agent's purpose." *Confusion* is a mental state "not seeing things as they are." *Helplessness* is "a state of dependency on another"—in this case on government programs rather than on God.

Through her structure of demonic entities, Jezebel has succeeded in supplanting worship and faith in God with confusion and dependency on government resulting in *generational poverty* in those loyal to her. Generational poverty, Black genocide, and hopelessness are *systemic*. High school dropouts and burgeoning prisons are the result of misplaced loyalty, trust, and dependence on Democratic-inspired government programs.

> There is a way which seems right to a man. But its
> end is the way of death. (Proverbs 14:12)

Tolerating Jezebel

The tragic consequences of misplaced trust are evident. However, in speaking to the Church at Thyatira, *the Lord holds the Church responsible*. He didn't reprimand Jezebel for her deception and seduction. That's her nature. He holds the one who *tolerates* Jezebel responsible.

In 1 Kings 21 we read the account of Ahab's desire for Naboth's orchard next door to the king's residence. Naboth wouldn't sell, so Queen Jezebel set up a sting operation with false witnesses and a trumped-up charge against Naboth to steal his land and murder him. Jezebel is the guilty party. However, when God sent the prophet Elijah to deliver His word to the guilty party, He sent Elijah to Ahab.

> Jesus didn't reprimand Jezebel for her deception and seduction. That's her nature. He holds the one who tolerates Jezebel responsible.

> "Arise, go down to meet Ahab king of Israel, who is
> in Samaria; behold, he is in the vineyard of Naboth
> where he has gone down to take possession of it. You
> shall speak to him, saying, 'Thus says the LORD,
> "Have you murdered and also taken possession?"
> And you shall speak to him, saying, 'Thus says the
> LORD, "In the place where the dogs licked up the
> blood of Naboth the dogs will lick up your blood,
> even yours...." Of Jezebel also has the LORD spoken,
> saying, 'The dogs will eat Jezebel in the district of
> Jezreel.'" (1 Kings 21:18-19, 23)

Queen Jezebel couldn't have exerted governmental authority without the cooperation or acquiescence of King Ahab, but God holds Ahab responsible. That brings us to the Republican Party.

The Ahab Structure Behind the Republican Party

Revelation 2:18-29 is the letter written to the Church at Thyatira. It is a picture of the Ahab Structure. This scripture passage is in the context of government. The reward for overcoming in verses 26 and 27 is "power over the nations—He shall *rule* [governmental rule] them with a rod of iron." Even the concept of *ruling with a rod of iron* is anathema to most Republicans. How can I say it? Most Republicans are *moral* but a lot of them are not strong. Many times they are weak and they give in to the Jezebel structure hiding behind the Democratic Party.

What the Lord Commends in the Church of Thyatira

- Your works, your love (in the KJV *charity*), your service, your faith, your patience, and your perseverance.

- You're better at the last than at the first.

- You're excelling in virtue.

The Republican Platform excels in virtue. The Republican Platform supports individual responsibility, less government, lower taxes, school prayer, the personhood and protection of unborn babies, school choice (educational options for parents to send their children to the private religious or public school of their choice with funding following the child), and traditional marriage between one man and one woman. Not all, but many Republican office holders are dedicated Christians and fully support the Republican Platform on all of these issues.

The Republican Party, however, is made up of three distinct groups of people:

- Fiscal conservatives who support limited government and low taxes.

- Anti-terrorists and strong national defense proponents. Before terrorism struck America, this segment consisted of anti-communist Republicans, such as Governor Arnold Schwarzenegger of California. Schwarzenegger experienced life behind the Iron Curtain. When he came to America, he supported the party that was most openly anti-Communist, which was the Republican Party. He is neither a fiscal nor a social conservative, but he is a Republican.

- Social conservatives who support the sanctity of human life, traditional marriage, school prayer, the posting of the Ten Commandments, and school choice. Social conservatives, for the most part, are also fiscal conservatives, anti-terrorists, and support a strong national defense. Of course, virtually all

Americans support the military, but Republicans, more than Democrats, support military action against nations who harbor terrorists.

What the Lord Condemns in the Church of Thyatira

- You *allow* that woman Jezebel—you *tolerate*—"to be done without prohibition, hindrance, or contradiction"—you *let*—"to give opportunity— not to forbid or prevent—allow or failure to prevent."

- God names the big sin as *tolerance*. The political left demonizes intolerance so much that those who courageously stand for biblical, moral values are labeled intolerant, homophobic or uncompassionate.

- By *not confronting, allowing* and *not prohibiting* Jezebel, weak leaders actually *partner with* and *empower* her to do her deceiving, her manipulating and her murdering. They *authorize by acquiescing*. By *giving in*, they *empower* the Jezebel Structure.

A Passive Spirit

Ahab is a study in contradictions. He is a strong military leader yet weak spiritually. He surrenders and yields to intimidation.

Ahab's big sin was passivity. Sometimes we pin things on spiritual apathy, but the correct word is passivity. There's a difference. Whereas *apathy* is a lack of interest, *passivity* is a lack of action. Francis Frangipane clarifies it in his excellent book, *This Day We Fight—Breaking the Stronghold of a Passive Spirit*.[4] Frangipane guided my thoughts on the three kings below.

Three familiar instances in the Bible demonstrate what happens when one is under the influence of a passive spirit.

- After King Joash was given arrows and commanded to strike the ground by the prophet Elisha, he struck the ground only three times and stopped.

  So the man of God was angry with him and said, "You should have struck five or six times, then you would have struck Aram [Syria] until you would have destroyed it! But now you shall strike Aram only three times." (2 Kings 13:19)

- King David stayed home one spring "at the time when kings go out to battle" (2 Samuel 11:1-17). The enemy used that time when David should have been on the battlefield to set him up for adultery with Bathsheba and the eventual murder of her husband to cover up the sin and resulting pregnancy. Not only did King David stay home when he should have been on the battlefield, but he was actually napping while his men were fighting.

  Now *when evening came* David *arose from his bed* and walked around on the roof of the king's house, and from the roof he saw a woman bathing; and the woman was very beautiful in appearance. (2 Samuel 11:2, emphasis mine)

- King Ahab allowed his wife Queen Jezebel to use his authority as king to bring in the worship of Baal and Asherah. King Ahab was not *weak*. He was a strong military leader, but when it came to religion and morality, he was *passive*. He authorized idolatry by his acquiescence.

It's interesting that all three of these examples are *governmental*. King Joash was passive about acting fully and passionately about a prophetic word. King David was passive about his duty and his personal purity. King Ahab was passive about his wife's use of his authority to break God's commandment *to have no other god before Me*. Their passivity resulted in loss in battle, the death of a child and judgment upon himself, his wife and his descendants.

Webster's definition of *passive* is "receptive to outside impressions or influences; lacking in energy or will; tending not to take an active or dominant part when induced by an outside agency; receiving or enduring without resistance; submissive or existing; or occurring without being active, open, or direct."

The kings above were passive toward the prophetic word, their responsibility to go to war and the establishment of idolatry. *The Church is passive toward government and political involvement.* They may see it as political and not moral. Cindy Jacobs, in assessing the state of our nation, wrote, "In the early '60s God poured out His Spirit on the Church, but we were so busy with wonderful revival that we retreated from government. Essentially we gave the government to the humanists and atheists. In 1962, for instance, we slumbered while the Supreme Court took prayer and Bible reading out of our schools."[5]

> The Church is passive toward government and political involvement. They may see it as political and not moral.

Our passivity caused the court cases that removed prayer from our public schools to remain, causing the protective wall around the

United States, our schools and our government to crumble. The very next year President John Kennedy was assassinated in Dallas. The country mourned but the protective walls were not restored.

Not only are many Christians passive toward civic involvement, some Republicans are *passive* where same-sex marriage and the GLBT agenda is concerned. President George W. Bush certainly was as I'll detail in the next chapter. *Why*? They don't want to seem uncaring or judgmental. Many times I'm embarrassed by Republicans on TV or in print who speak about governmental issues. I may agree with the person on the issue, but I disagree with the tone and the name-calling. Those of us in the *prayer movement* who have been influenced by Ed Silvoso understand the *power of blessing*—to bless those who curse us (Luke 6:28) and to even love our enemies (Luke 6:27). Our heart is to reach out to people trapped in sin of any kind, including the GLBT lifestyle. We want people to see the compassionate face of Jesus. We're put off by angry-sounding, judgmental rhetoric. We believe in *blessing people*, even *certified sinners*. We believe in *the grace of God*. We not only believe in it, we've received the love of God that covered a multitude of sins in our own lives (1 Peter 4:8).

The Separation of Church and State

Some of us may have bought into the doctrine of the *separation of church and state*, although the concept of the separation of church and state is *foreign to our Constitution*. We may have been *influenced* by those who want to take the free exercise of religion out of the public square. "Exercise your religion in the church of your choice, but leave religious expression and moral values out of the public debate." That has basically been the stance of the Democratic Party, although not all Democrats. However, this position is against the belief of the Founding Fathers and the First Amendment to the U.S. Constitution, which states, "Congress shall make no law respecting an establishment of religion, or prohibiting the free exercise thereof...."

What the Founders meant by *religion* was a certain Christian *denomination*, not Christianity versus Islam, etc. England's official religion was Anglican. Spain's official religion was Catholic. Not at any time did the Founders mean anything other than a Christian denomination. They all believed in the God of Abraham, Isaac, and Jacob. Of 175 Founding Fathers, their church affiliation was: Episcopalian and Anglican 88, Presbyterian 30, Congregationalist 27, Quaker 7, Dutch Reformed 6, Lutheran 5, Catholic 3, Huguenot 3, Unitarian 3, Methodist 2 and Calvinist 1.[6] Not knowing our history can cause us to be timid about our faith and values.

And none of us, including Republican elected officials, want to be called intolerant, a bigot, uncompassionate, racist, or other names that sound like we don't love people.

---

[1] Dr. Alveda C. King, "Alveda: Why Did People Vote for Barack Obama?" American Outreach for Priests for Life, December 22, 2009, http://www.youtube.com/watch?v=LQJ6HCqUgQc.

[2] Dick Tripp,"Four Major Worldviews," *Exploring Christianity — Truth,* http://www.christianity.co.nz/truth2.htm.

[3] All definitions are taken from Merriam-Webster Online Dictionary, http://www.merriam-webster.com.

[4] Francis Frangipane, This Day We Fight – Breaking the Stronghold of a Passive Spirit, (Grand Rapids, MI: Chosen Books, 2005).

[5] Jacobs, 56.

[6] "Religious Affiliation of the Founding Fathers of the United States of America." http://www.adherents.com/gov/Founding_Fathers_Religion.html.

Chapter 13

TOLERANCE—
VIRTUE OR SIN?

TOLERANCE IS A VIRTUE THAT MOST AMERICANS VALUE. We *should* be tolerant of differences. We should even *celebrate* our cultural differences and in the diverse heritage of our nation. But there are some things that God does *not* want us to tolerate. He spelled-out those things to the Church of Thyatira (see Chapter 12). The Lord admonished the Church not to tolerate Jezebel. Ahab acquiesced to Jezebel and thus ceded his authority to her.

Ahab Acquiesces to Elijah

While studying Ahab and the verses of scripture relating to him, I found a startling piece of information. Not only did Ahab not impede Queen Jezebel from killing the prophets of God, he didn't try to dissuade Elijah from killing the prophets of Baal. Elijah told Ahab to gather the prophets of Baal and Asherah to Mt. Carmel:

> "Now then send and gather to me all Israel at Mount
> Carmel, together with 450 prophets of Baal and 400
> prophets of the Asherah, who eat at Jezebel's table."

So Ahab sent a message among all the sons of Israel
and brought the prophets together at Mount Carmel.
(1 Kings 18:19-20)

Notice that Ahab *brought* the false prophets to Mount Carmel. *And* he was there throughout the confrontation between God and Baal. He was still there after Elijah killed the false prophets as indicated in I Kings 18:38-41 when Elijah told Ahab to "go up, eat and drink; for there is the sound of the roar of a heavy shower" (verse 41).

King Ahab raced home to tattle on Elijah to Jezebel because he wanted her to do something about it. Later Ahab acquiesced to Elijah just like he did to Jezebel. He was passive toward both good and evil. We don't know his true feelings because he remained silent. Ahab told Jezebel what Elijah did, but he said nothing to Elijah. He opposed Elijah behind his back to Jezebel, but he didn't have the courage to stand against Elijah to his face. Ahab succumbed to Jezebel as well as to Elijah. He didn't have the backbone to confront either evil or good or to make a stand in either camp. (Some Republicans talk about issues they oppose to their constituents but are silent and acquiesce when it comes time to confront the issue where they can do something about it.)

When Ahab didn't stop Jezebel from welcoming the prophets of Baal and Asherah who were setting up their idolatrous worship, he actually *authorized it by his acquiescence.* In Revelation 2, Jesus didn't reprimand Jezebel, but he did reprimand the Church for not stopping *that woman Jezebel* from teaching and deceiving others into accepting and participating in immorality. The Church is responsible just as Ahab is responsible.

Ahab surrenders and yields to intimidation. Republicans fear labels such as intolerant, homophobic, racist, and uncaring. They acquiesce, compromise, and give their authority away under the constant pounding by Democrats and the fear of what people will think and the media will write. Many Republicans oppose government spending, abortion, and same-sex marriage but at times lack the courage to force such issues to a vote. Fear creates an Ahab and makes him tolerant of Jezebel. He is easily enticed and controlled by forces making up the Jezebel structure, e.g. trusting government to meet needs, the shedding of innocent blood and immorality.

> Fear creates an Ahab and makes him tolerant of Jezebel.

(In the summer of 2010 when this is written, Democrats have a strong majority in the House and a 59 to 41 vote in the Senate. It is impossible for Republicans to block votes or bring something to the floor in this situation. However, when they were in power with the Presidency plus both Houses in the first six years of President George W. Bush's tenure, they did not use their majorities to restrict the growth of government or to pass a federal marriage amendment. In fact, government grew under their stewardship. That's the reason Democrats gained power in 2006 in both the Senate and the House, two years before President Obama was elected.)

Another characteristic of Ahab that we can see in the Republican Party is that it's hard for them to follow through to victory. They compromise. They don't have a *killer instinct*. It's the same way that King Ahab reacted when the Lord told him to destroy the Arameans. When King Ben-hadab saw that they were losing, he said to his men, "Behold now, we have heard that the kings of the house of Israel are *merciful kings,* please let us put sackcloth on our loins and ropes on our heads, and go out to the king of Israel; perhaps he will save your life" (1 Kings 20:31, emphasis mine). King Ben-hadab was right. Ahab showed him mercy and did not destroy him as the Lord had directed through His prophets. And the Lord pronounced judgment on Ahab "because you have let go out of your hand the man whom I had devoted to destruction" (1 Kings 20:42). We should be merciful to those trapped in sin, but we must not be merciful to Jezebel or the governmental demonic structure she's empowering.

We see this misplaced mercy operating in Republicans in general, but not in every individual, just as the Jezebel structure is not successful in restricting every Democrat. However, the further you get up the ladder in Washington, D. C. or state government, the harder it is to withstand the power of the Ahab structure if you're a Republican and the Jezebel structure if you're a Democrat.

A case in point is the health care debate of 2009 regarding pro-life Democrats. Democratic Congressman Bart Stupak from Michigan was successful in getting an amendment to the House version of the Health Care Bill saying that federal funds cannot be used to fund abortion. Democratic Senator Ben Nelson of Nebraska introduced a similar amendment in the Senate, which was tabled by Democratic Senator Barbara Boxer of California. The vote against tabling the amendment was a pro-abortion vote, which passed 54 to 45. The two Maine Republicans, Senators Olympia Snowe and Susan Collins, voted pro-abortion and seven Democrats: Senators Evan Bayh (D-IN), Robert Casey (D-PA), Kent Conrad (D-ND), Byron Dorgan (D-ND), Ted Kaufman (D-DE), Ben Nelson (D-NE) and Mark Pryor (D-AR)— joined 40 Republicans to vote pro-life. *However*, when the vote came up in the Senate to move the Health Care Bill to the floor of the Senate for a vote (which essentially assured that abortion funding in the bill would pass because the same 54 who opposed the pro-life amendment would pass the bill with abortion in it), those seven pro-life Democrats caved in to Democratic pressure and voted to move the Health Care Bill to the floor of the Senate for a vote *despite* the provision for government-funded abortion in the bill. A great amount of promises, arm-twisting, and downright bribes caused the one holdout Senator Ben Nelson of Nebraska to succumb to pressure to become the sixtieth vote to move the legislation containing mandatory abortion coverage in the government-condoned insurance to the floor for a vote. Senator Nelson and the other so-called pro-life senators all received a huge payoff for their votes. FOX NEWS documents the payoffs in an article, *The Price Is Right? Payoffs for Senators Typical in Health Care Bill,*[1] printed in full in Appendix B.

The so-called pro-life Democratic Senators hid behind the process saying that they voted for the pro-life amendment and voted against the health care bill when it came to the floor for a vote. *But* the whole truth of the situation is that their vote to move the bill to the floor for a vote was a pro-abortion vote cloaked in the process of the Senate which required a two-thirds majority to move any bill to the floor for a vote.

This scenario solidifies my point that it's very difficult to vote consistently pro-life if you're a Democrat. The Democratic Party uses fear and intimidation against social conservatives in their own ranks. The money promised to districts if they'd just support the Health Care Bill set a new low in coercion and bribes to get all the Democrats to tow the line—no matter what their districts thought about it. In this case, the pro-life Democratic senators acquiesced. Jezebel succeeded in keeping her subjects in line and pushing through legislation that will cripple the United States for years to come.

Although the Republican Party Platform is full of virtue, many individual Republicans tolerate what the platform does not. Take former evangelical President George W. Bush. Here are just a few of his actions that align with King Ahab's tolerance of Jezebel.

- He was the first Republican President to appoint an open homosexual to high office— Scott Evertz to the White House Office of National AIDS Policy. [2]

- After the Islamic terrorist attack on the Twin Towers on 9/11/ 2001, President Bush invited 50 ambassadors from Muslim countries for a traditional meal and prayer at the White House in November 2001 to mark the start of Ramadan. A Republican President was the first to invite Muslims to pray in the White House. President Barack Obama continued the celebration of Ramadan in the White House, but it was started by a Republican President.[3]

- President and Mrs. Bush bowed before the Meiji Shrine in Tokyo.[4]

- President Bush "removed his shoes, entered a mosque and praised Islam for inspiring 'countless individuals to lead lives of honesty, integrity and morality.' For the second time since the September 11 terrorist attacks, the president yesterday visited Washington's oldest mosque, the Islamic Center, where Muslims from 75 nations gather to worship. Mrs. Bush marked the end of the Muslim holy month of Ramadan by praising Islam as a hopeful religion of mercy and tolerance." [5]

- President Bush outraged evangelicals by stating that he believes that Christians and Muslims worship the same god.[6]

- In 2004 President Bush campaigned in favor of a Marriage Amendment to the U.S. Constitution that says that marriage is between one man and one woman. However, when he was elected, he said no more about it. If he had put as much importance on it as he did in reforming Social Security, the Marriage Amendment would have passed through Congress. He even said on several occasions that he supported civil unions, which give the same rights as marriage to same-sex couples.[7]

- President Bush proved over and over again that he was an Ahab.

So what should an individual or political party do that *yields* instead of taking action?

Dismantling Jezebel and Ahab Structures

What should an individual or a political party do to extract from a Jezebel or Ahab structure? *Repent!* Did you know that even Ahab repented?

After Jezebel succeeded in having Naboth murdered and his land confiscated for Ahab, the Lord spoke to Elijah. The passage is long, but it's important.

> The word of the LORD came to Elijah the Tishbite,
> saying, "Arise, go down to meet Ahab king of Israel,
> who is in Samaria; behold, he is in the vineyard of
> Naboth where he has gone down to take possession
> of it. You shall speak to him, saying, 'Thus says the
> LORD, "Have *you* murdered and also taken posses-

sion?" [Actually it was Jezebel who had Naboth murdered, but God attributes the sin to Ahab here.] And you shall speak to him, saying, 'Thus says the LORD, "In the place where the dogs licked up the blood of Naboth the dogs will lick up your blood, even yours.

"Behold, I will bring evil upon you, and will utterly sweep you away, and will cut off from Ahab every male, both bond and free in Israel... because of the provocation with which you have provoked Me to anger, and because you have made Israel sin.

"Of Jezebel also has the LORD spoken, saying, 'The dogs will eat Jezebel in the district of Jezreel. The one belonging to Ahab, who dies in the city, the dogs will eat, and the one who dies in the field, the birds of heaven will eat.'"

Surely there was no one like Ahab who sold himself to do evil in the sight of the LORD because Jezebel his wife incited him. He acted very abominably in following idols, according to all that the Amorites had done, whom the LORD cast out before the sons of Israel. *It came about when Ahab heard these words, that he tore his clothes and put on sackcloth and fasted, and he lay in sackcloth and went about despondently.* Then the word of the LORD came to Elijah the Tishbite, saying, "Do you see how Ahab has humbled himself before Me? Because he has humbled himself before Me, I will not bring the evil in his days, but I

will bring the evil upon his house in his son's days."
(1 Kings 21:17–29, emphases mine)

Ahab repented and God relented. The Lord noticed Ahab's repentance, was touched by it, and called it to Elijah's attention. Then He told Elijah that He wouldn't bring the judgment on him that He had told Elijah to prophesy over him. The judgment would wait until the next generation. Is it hard to fathom how far God's forgiveness reaches? It is for me.

Here's another important fact that goes against our nature. The Lord didn't require restitution for what Ahab had done. He didn't even tell Ahab to give Naboth's land back to his family or at the very least pay them for the stolen land. He simply forgave Ahab and deferred the judgment He had planned on to the next generation. I guess we could say that restitution was the judgment pronounced upon Ahab's descendants, but there was no monetary restitution.

We can all repent of our false beliefs and ways. Ahab repented and so did Democratic, four-term Governor George Wallace of Alabama. Governor Wallace opposed public school segregation and tried to block Black students from entering the University of Alabama in June 1963, as well as four separate elementary schools in Huntsville in September 1963. In his January 1963 inaugural address, he shouted, "Segregation now, segregation tomorrow and segregation forever."[8]

In the late 1970s, Governor Wallace announced that he had become a born-again Christian and he apologized for his segregationist views. He didn't just make a public apology, but he also called Black civil rights leaders to personally apologize to them. He said that while he had once sought power and glory, he realized he needed to seek love and forgiveness. He stated, "I was wrong. Those days are over and they ought to be over." His last term as Governor (1983–1987) saw a record number of Black appointments to government positions.[9] Isn't it amazing what God can do when we repent and turn to Him?

Pray with me.

> *Father, it's hard to understand Your mercy, Your grace, and Your forgiveness. I come to humble myself before You and to repent for the times that I have acquiesced because of passivity. Forgive me for not taking action and making my voice heard on important issues of the day. Forgive me for being merciful when you want strength and decisive action. I ask You to forgive Republicans for backing down when they need to stand up, Democrats for caving in to the demands of their Party, and Independents for staying out of the process so they won't have to wear a label. Lord, give us courage to engage, in Jesus' name.*

Now Is the Time to Dismantle False Structures

Now is the time to remove false structures and obstacles that hinder God's justice at the governmental gates. In fact, God commissions us to prepare the way before Him.

> Go through, go through the gates; clear the way for the people. Build up, build up the highway; remove the stones. [Take out the hindrances. Remove the structures built to hinder the procession of God's justice and righteousness—the advancement of God's kingdom.] Lift up a banner [a standard of justice and righteousness—God's rule] for the people.
> (Isaiah 62:10, parentheses mine)

First let's deal with our own lives before we look at the broader question of how to dismantle demonic networks in political parties or regions. Even in our own personal lives, it's not a simple *one, two, three.*

Realizing that you've been deceived and manipulated by forces bent on your destruction is unsettling. This may be how you're feeling at this moment. The things you've read are overwhelming. You wish they weren't true, but the Holy Spirit is witnessing to your spirit that they are. You have been deceived.

> Deception is the hardest thing to recognize in yourself because being deceived is thinking you're right when you're wrong.

Deception is the hardest thing to recognize in yourself because being deceived is thinking you're right when you're wrong. It takes the truth of God, the light of His Word and the grace of God to unveil the facts and to enable you to receive them. I know firsthand what it feels like to realize you've been deceived. Over 30 years ago we were in a church that gradually got into deception. It started as a thriving congregation with many receiving salvation, as well as outgrowing two church buildings. Sound teaching was given in how to mature in Christ. But gradually we began to be deceived. *It's the enemy's plan to make us go too far in legalism if he can't get us to sin.* We eventually sold our house and gave all of the money to the church. All of us lived together in our church building in separate bedrooms. The women wore long dresses and head coverings and couldn't pray or minister, even to other women.

Then the Lord woke me up and showed me through a Christian magazine that we were in deception—the entire May 1979 issue was devoted to *Cults*. In one article it gave a list of 14 characteristics of cults. The writer said, "If you're any one of these, you're in some measure of deception." We were *every one of them*! I was shocked. Once we left the church and people we loved, we sought to know the truth about where we had been deceived. We sometimes felt we were *walking against the light*. It took several months for me to put on a street-length dress and years to wear pants. When I cut my hair and began to wear make-up, it was hard not to feel guilty. It was easier to be loyal to the teachings of legalism and deception than it was to act on the truth.

---

[1] "The Price is Right? Payoff for Senators Typical in Health Care Bill," December 21, 2009, FOXNews.com, http://www.foxnews.com/politics/2009/12/21/price-right-payoffs-senators-typical-health-care.

[2] Groening, Chad and Jody Brown, "Christian Groups Disturbed by Bush's Choice of Homosexual to Head AIDS Office," *Agape Press*, April 11, 2001, http://www.apfn.net/messageboard/01-24-05/discussion.cgi.41.html scroll down to article or search for Scott Evertz

[3] Ben Fenton, "Muslims to Pray in the White House," *Telegraph.co.uk*, November 16, 2001 http://www.telegraph.co.uk/news/worldnews/northamerica/usa/1362594/Muslims-to-pray-in-the-White-House.html.

[4] "Bushes Take in Archery Show at Shrine, *The Japan Times Online*, February 19, 2002, http://search.japantimes.co.jp/cgi-bin/nn20020219a4.html.

[5] Bill Sammon, "Bush Praises Islam for its 'Morality,'" *The Washington Times*, December 6, 2002, http://www.chuckbaldwinlive.com/bushlovesislam.html.

6 "Evangelicals outraged over Bush's 'Same God' Remark," *World Net Daily*, November 24, 2003, http://www.wnd.com/?pageId=21965.

[7] Bush Marriage Stance Not Clear," *The Washington Times*, December 17, 2003, http://washingtontimes.com/news/2003/dec/17/20031217-115104-4009r.

[8] http://en.wikipedia.org/wiki/George_Wallace.

[9] Ibid.

Chapter 14

DISMANTLING UNHOLY STRUCTURES

SEVERAL YEARS AGO IN A TOWN IN SOUTH TEXAS, I convened a meeting of key Black pastors and leaders to meet with Susan Weddington and David Barton while they were Chairman and Vice-Chairman of the Republican Party of Texas. David gave a presentation about some of the things I've shared in Chapter 5, including the Democrats' record on civil rights. One of my dear pastor friends made this statement, "The first time I voted Republican, I wept in the booth. I still can't tell my mother. I thought, *I sure hope I'm not betraying my race and voting for the ship that brought us here.*"

Sometimes walking in the truth feels like betrayal. But many times it's unfounded loyalty. That's the title of a book I highly recommend to you written by my dear friend, Rev. Wayne Perryman from Seattle. It's called *Unfounded Loyalty—An In-depth Look into the Blind Love Affair between Blacks and Democrats*, "A Fact-Finding Investigation from 1832 to 2004 covering: The Democrats' Racist Past, The Republicans' Quest for Equality, and the Power of Christianity on the African American Culture."

Rev. Perryman had no interest in writing a book about Blacks and Democrats. However, a member of his youth group asked him, "Why are we [Black Christians] Democrats and White Christians Republicans?" Rev. Perryman gave a glib answer, but then the Lord urged him to research the differences in the two political parties so he could give an informed answer to his youth group. The result was astounding facts that he wrote in this book.[1] Rev. Perryman still does not call himself a Republican—or a Democrat, for that matter—but he is an advocate for knowing the truth and for voting your values. Rev. Perryman embraced the truth and acted on it.

There are three areas where unholy structures must be dismantled: on a personal level in your own life, on a strategic spiritual level, and on a national governmental area. In this book I will deal with the personal level and the strategic spiritual level. It will take another book to adequately deal with the governmental grassroots level, but I will touch on it in the next chapter.

ON THE PERSONAL LEVEL

Embrace the Truth

Align yourself with the truth you've read and ask God to give you grace to accept it. *Lord, I embrace Your truth. I trust You for grace to walk in the truth.* Begin your own study of history if you want to discover more facts. (Keep in mind that some so-called historical facts may be a point of view or an opinion that serve the agendas of the promoters of those facts. Check the cited references to see if the "facts" are from reliable original or secondary sources.)

Repent for Having Believed a Lie

Humble yourself before the Lord and ask Him to cleanse you from deception. Repentance removes the place we have given Satan in our lives. Isaiah 26:13 says, "Oh, Lord our God, masters besides You have had dominion over us, but by You only we make mention of Your name."

> *Lord, forgive me for believing a lie and allowing myself to*
> *be deceived. I repent and I take back any ground I may*
> *have given Satan through my deception.*

Prioritize Intimacy with God

Set aside time to worship, pray, and study God's Word in private. Delight yourself in the Lord. Focus your attention on the truth of God's Word. Trust Him to continue to cleanse you and to prepare you to be a part of dismantling structures outside your own life. Set yourself on a course of study to discover the truth. Ask the Lord to continue to show you areas of deception in your life.

> Thus says the Lord, "Let not the wise man glory in
> his wisdom. Let not the mighty man glory in his
> might, nor let the rich man glory in his riches. But let
> him who glories, glory in this, that he understands
> and knows Me, that I am the Lord, exercising lov-
> ingkindness, judgment and righteousness in the
> earth. For in these I delight," says the Lord. (Jere-
> miah 9:23)

> *Lord, it's my desire to know You. As I give You time and*
> *worship, open my eyes to who You really are. Teach me*
> *Your ways. I want to walk in Your truth, to worship You*

*in spirit and in truth and to please You in every area of
my life. Open my eyes to other areas of deception. Give me
wisdom and discernment to embrace the truth no matter
how painful it is.*

Engage in the Civic Arena

The way you engage is to register and vote in every election. You don't have to *wear the label* or *promote* a political party to engage in the party process.

Many Christians celebrate being *Independent*. You should be an *independent* voter in General Elections. Choose the person—either the Democrat or the Republican—who most closely aligns with your values. If you vote in the Republican (or Democratic) Primary and go to the precinct conventions (or caucuses), you don't have to vote for candidates in that party in the General Election. This is very important. Vote for the person of either party who most closely reflects

> Vote for the person of either party who most closely reflects your values.

your values. Some people think that if they consider themselves a Democrat that they must vote a straight Democratic ticket in the General Election. That is not true.

However, and this is so important, engage in one of the two political parties. Being an *Independent* and not voting in either the Democratic or Republican Primaries means that you are leaving the most basic choice to someone else. When you say you're an *Independent* and don't vote in either Primary Election, *you are not at the table.* Your values are not influencing the selection of either party's nominee. And by not engaging in the party process, your voice is not heard in forming the platform or choosing officers. It's important to bring your vote and influence to bear at the beginning of the process in one of the two main parties.

Below are some startling statistics.

- Only half the Christians in America who are eligible to vote are registered.

- Only half of those registered actually vote in General Presidential Elections held every four years.

- Sometimes little more than 10 percent vote in Primary Elections where the two political parties choose their nominees to face the other party in the General Election.

- And a shocking number... less than one percent of registered voters are engaged in the party process of either political party.

Remember, *the smaller the number of people involved, the more impact you can have with just a little organization.*

The rules are not the same in every state. Some states like Hawaii require you to join either the Democratic or Republican Party to be involved in party caucuses. In some states you must register as a Democrat or Republican before you can vote in a Primary Election. In states like Texas that have *open primaries,* you do not register by party. You just vote in either the Democratic or Republican Primary, and then you can attend that party's *precinct convention* at your polling place the evening of the Primary Election. The three most important words in politics are *just show up.* You don't have to know what to do

> The smaller the number of people involved, the more impact you can have with just a little organization.

at a *precinct convention*. Just show up, pay attention and try to get elected as a delegate to the next level. The first time you *show up*, you will be learning the process. After that, you can teach others.

ON THE STRATEGIC SPIRITUAL LEVEL
IN THE TWO POLITICAL PARTIES

There are three strategic instruments required at the spiritual level for dismantling structures in the two political parties:

- Expose the enemy by speaking the truth
- Call for the wailing women
- Worship (which I'll discuss in the next chapter)

Expose the Enemy by Speaking the Truth

Satan fears the truth. Wield the Sword of the Spirit, which is the Word of God (Ephesians 6:17) that the Lord has placed in your hand and in your mouth.

> For the word of God is living and active and sharper
> than any two-edged sword, and piercing as far as the
> division of soul and spirit, of both joints and marrow,
> and able to judge the thoughts and intentions of the
> heart. (Hebrews 4:12)

There have been very few times in my life when I have seen a vision. However, in May 2009 in Houston at a Dutch Sheets meeting, the Lord moved on me to go to the platform to pray. "I lift the skirts of Jezebel." After I prayed that and returned to my seat, I saw Jezebel's skirt lifted to expose tiny Baal, Asherah, and a few other spirits. There they were—small, cowering, trembling little spirits that were only ankle high on Jezebel's skinny legs. They were afraid to have the light of

God shine on them and be found out. They are not huge. Yes, they gain power by false worship, the shedding of innocent blood, broken covenants, and immorality. But compared to the power of God, the truth of God's Word, the name of Jesus, the blood of the Lamb and the word of our testimony, they are small. Remember, "The demons also believe, and shudder" (James 2:19).

The Word of God gives us perspective on the size of Satan's forces. "You are from God, little children, and have overcome them; because greater is He who is in you than he who is in the world" (1 John 4:4). The Spirit of the Lord is greater than any principality, power of darkness, or spiritual ruler in heavenly places. "And having spoiled principalities and powers, he [Jesus] made a shew [show] of them openly, triumphing over them in it" (Colossians 2:15, KJV). Jesus already defeated principalities and powers when He rose from the dead. The work is finished. Our part is to appropriate the finished work in own lives and in our nation.

Come in the Opposite Spirit

The opposite spirit of tolerance is confrontation. Refuse to tolerate or back down. Confront. Expose. Uncover. Make known.

> These things are the things you shall do: speak each
> man the truth to his neighbor. Give judgment in your
> gates for truth, justice and peace." (Zechariah 8:16)

Expose the ungodly *Jezebel structure* of economic dependence on government, condoning same-sex marriage, and promoting abortion. Expose the ungodly *Ahab structure* of fear, intimidation, tolerance, passivity, and compromise.

As Christian leaders, many have tried very hard to be nonpartisan—to not sound like Republicans. Your church or nonprofit organization cannot endorse candidates, but pastors don't lose their constitutional rights to free speech and to engage in the politi-

> Now is not the time for careful rhetoric. It's the time for truth and confrontation.

cal process just because they head up a nonprofit organization. Now is not the time for careful rhetoric. It's the time for truth and confrontation.

It goes without saying that some people are not going to like it. The weapons of fear and intimidation will be used against you, but it's time for truth and courage to prevail. You have the victory if you'll use your spiritual weapons. "They overcame him by the blood of the Lamb, the word of their testimony, and *they loved not their life to death*" (Revelation 12:11). Do not fear man, what people think or tarnishing your own reputation. Overcome.

Call for the Wailing Women

Please don't check out here—stay with me. This could be the most important piece in the strategy for dismantling structures. Calling for the wailing women comes from Jeremiah. Jeremiah was a prophet whom the Lord used during the reign of King Josiah and afterward. Part of his calling was to pull down structures.

> The word of the Lord came to me, saying, "Before I formed you in the womb, I knew you. Before I sanctified you, I ordained you a prophet to the nations."
> Then said I, "Ah Lord God! Behold, I cannot speak, for I am a youth." But the Lord said to me, "Do not

say, 'I am a youth,' for you shall go to all to whom I
send you, and whatever I command you, you shall
speak. Do not be afraid of their faces [don't be an
Ahab], for I am with you to deliver you. Behold, I
have put My words in your mouth. See, I have this
day set you over the nations and over the kingdoms,
to root out and to pull down, to destroy and to throw
down [ungodly structures], to build and to plant."
(Jeremiah 1:5-10, parentheses mine)

The Lord instructed Jeremiah to go to certain places and prophesy
what he was told to say. Besides speaking the word of the Lord at specific times and designated places, the only other instruction the Lord
gave Jeremiah was to call for the wailing women.

Thus says the Lord of hosts, "Consider and call for
the mourning women that they may come. And send
for the skillful wailing women that they may come.
Let them make haste and take up a wailing for us
that our eyes may run with tears and our eyelids
gush with water. Teach your daughters wailing and
everyone her neighbor a lamentation. For death has
come through our windows, has entered our palaces,
to *kill off the children*—no longer to be outside—*and
the young men*—no longer on the streets." (Jeremiah
9:17-21, emphases mine)

The wailing women were professional mourners who wailed at
funerals. This call for wailing women, which today would be seasoned
intercessors, was directly related to the death of children. It was because children were dying and young men were no longer on the

streets. Today we have the lives of millions of unborn babies extinguished in the womb. Many young men in the inner cities of America die on the streets or end up in prison. Either way they are *no longer on the streets.*

What do we do about the situation? What do we do about the structure that supports abortion, keeps inner city children in failing, unsafe public schools, and perpetuates systemic poverty by devising government programs that lead to the loss of initiative as well as generational dependence on government?

Some things in the natural can be done in the civic arena, and I'll touch on them in the next chapter. However, calling for the wailing women is very important. This is where God has moved the most powerfully as I've shared this teaching in various places.

> Wailing is actually mourning and repenting for the sins of our nation and for allowing ungodly structures to stand.

Wailing is actually mourning and repenting for the sins of our nation and for allowing ungodly structures to stand. We've repented and confessed, but the sin of tolerating Jezebel structures has not reached our core—our hearts, our emotions. We've not been stirred to mourning and wailing. Now is the time to call for the wailing women. Mourn for young men in prison, babies murdered in the womb, and children without fathers. And, it's not just women who are called to wail. God also calls the shepherds, the spiritual leaders.

> Wail, shepherds, and cry! Roll about in the ashes,
> you leaders of the flock....A voice of the cry of the

shepherds and a wailing of the leaders to the flock
will be heard. (Jeremiah 25:34, 36)

Repent for allowing these structures to stand and rule over us! But do more than repent. Let it touch your core and *WAIL*!

Two Confirmations

When I've shared this portion of a strategy that the Lord gave me for dismantling ungodly structures, two huge confirmations have been given to me. One came at New Life Christian Center in San Antonio the weekend before the November 2004 election. I wasn't going to emphasize the wailing women because I'd already convened a very small, strategic group of intercessors who had come to our office that very day to wail for the election. However, when I finished speaking, Dr. LaSalle Vaughn, pastor of New Life Christian Center, came to the platform, "Alice, when you talked about calling for the wailing women, something went off in my spirit." He then proceeded to call several key women to the altar. He charged them to lead us in wailing. As the congregation wailed, I sensed that we broke through. Wailing didn't seem to be foreign to this mostly Black congregation. I learned later that wailing is a part of the heritage of the Black Church.

The other confirmation was in 2005 in Denton, Texas, at *Starting the Year Off Right Conference* convened by Dr. Chuck Pierce and held at North Texas University. This was a multicultural gathering, although most of the attendees were White. I was speaking on the Jezebel/Ahab structures and how to dismantle them. I didn't really know how to proceed, but I sensed that I was to talk with Joan Swallow, wife of Dr. Jay Swallow, so I approached Joan during a break. With the Trail of Tears[2] and all that Native Americans have suffered since the White man came to these shores, I thought they probably knew about mourning and wailing. Joan told me, "We sometimes go into travail in intercession, but we always wail at funerals. Even though we know they're in heaven, we still miss them." That's what the scripture describes—wailing for children that are no more.

That was the information I needed.

I asked Joan to gather some Native women from Oklahoma who also attended the conference. When I finished teaching, I called for the wailing women to come to the platform. Others came forward and even some Native Americans from Alaska. I asked Falma to come up. Many other Black intercessors came as well. In addition, Rosie Díaz, Thelma Rendon, and Mary Alice Martinez, who are Sephardic Jews from my church in San Antonio, responded to the call.

When the women had drawn near, I asked Joan to lead us in wailing. Since I had also spoken about *wailing shepherds*, Chuck exhorted the one thousand people in attendance to wail. Joan and her Native women led us. The sound was incredible.

A Sound That Moves God's Heart

There is a cry that the Lord turns aside to hear, as He did when He called Moses at the burning bush. He said, "Behold now *the cry* of the sons of Israel has come to me" (Exodus 3:9), and "I have seen the affliction of my people and have given heed *to their cry*" (Exodus 3:7 emphases mine).

I don't know what it is about sound, but there is a sound that moves God's heart. It's a sound that's full of passion and mourning. It's not a nice sweet song or a well-worded prayer. It's a wail that catches His attention and moves Him to wage war against the spirit of death. The shedding of innocent blood empowers evil spirits, and wailing has a part in dismantling their power.

After the time of wailing at the conference in Denton, Kay Scribner, an intercessor from the Dallas/Fort Worth Metroplex approached me. She had seen a vision while the women were wailing and wrote it down for me. Here's what it said.

> Alice—for your consideration. When we were in intercession yesterday during your session and went into the wailing women portion, I heard and saw the following vision: I saw a German concentration camp and a host of women outside the compound, next to the extermination building. They were looking to heaven and wailing for the loss of their children and their families.
>
> There was a "hearing" from heaven of their cries that was set apart by God to connect with what happened here yesterday. In the joining of the cries, there was a dismantling of the unholy alliance between Hitler and the woman who founded Planned Parenthood [Margaret Sanger]. That alliance had given power to the enemy that was not able to be broken and set down until the connection of wailing women here with the wails of those *held* for that moment.
>
> There was an incredible synergy in the release of those cries that is greater than we realized.

As I read the note, the Lord took me back to Auschwitz, a concentration camp in Poland that I visited in March 2002 with a group from

The Life Chapel led by Dell Sanchez. I knew before I left to go on the trip that the Lord would have me repent for what the Nazis did to millions of Jews because part of my heritage is German.

When we arrived at Auschwitz, I knew this was the place. The grounds looked like a college campus with beautiful red brick buildings and manicured lawns. For anyone climbing downstairs to *the showers*, nothing would have been alarming. As we descended the stairs to the basement, a somber silence settled on our group.

It wasn't an easy thing to be obedient at Auschwitz. I'm usually quick to repent because I know the power of identificational repentance. But by the time we got to the gas chambers that looked like showers in the basement, the silence was deafening. We had viewed rooms full of the belongings of some of Hitler's victims. Through glass walls you could see one room filled with piles of eye glasses, one with mounds of children's shoes, one with adult shoes, one with women's hair and one with Jewish tallits or prayer shawls. In the basement I was nervous, but the Lord was insistent.

Inside one of the gas chambers I got on my knees and began to repent. First softly and then weeping. Then I lay face-down on the cold concrete with my arms stretched out to the side, and I heard a wail. It was loud and sounded far away. I wondered who it was. Then I realized it was coming out of me. It shocked me. I don't remember if anyone joined in my cry. I just remember the loud wail that came from deep, deep inside.

One of the most amazing things in Denton was that Mary Alice, Rosie, and Thelma, who were on the platform wailing, had been in that gas chamber at Auschwitz. Kay's vision connected the wails of

Jewish women with the wails of Native, Sephardic Jewish, Black, White, and Asian women wailing in Denton.

The Lord connected the prayers of Jewish women wailing for their children to the wails led by Native American women to begin to break the power of Black genocide and to dethrone Jezebel.

That Sunday during the worship service at Glory of Zion Church in Denton, Cindy Jacobs was ministering. She spoke about Jezebel. At one point she called me to the front to prophesy over me. Among other things she said was, "Alice, God has given you authority over Jezebel. You're on the right track. Don't back up."

Then later in her message about Jezebel she declared, "Jezebel was dethroned this weekend." Cindy was not in the meeting where I spoke and didn't know about the wailing or what happened before she arrived. It was a huge confirmation for me.

When Is It Enough?

So how many times do we need to call for the wailing women? I don't know, but I know the power of it. When the truth is presented, the wailing brings breakthrough. As Jeremiah prophesied and called for the wailing women, King Josiah tore down the altars of Baal, Asherah and other false gods. King Josiah commissioned the repairs of the temple, the Book of the Law was found and a twelve-year revival ensued.

For the structures to be dismantled, revival to break through, and transformation to begin, some strategically-placed wailing that deals with political structures must take place in days ahead.

> *Lord, we ask for Your direction and strategy about where*
> *to go and when to call for the wailing women.*

1 Wayne Perryman, *Unfounded Loyalty — An In-depth Look into the Blind Love Affair between Blacks and Democrats*, (Hara Publishing Group: Seattle, WA, 2004), inside cover.

2 The forced relocation of Cherokees and other tribes, primarily the Chickasaw, Choctaw, Creek and Seminole, from Georgia to west of the Mississippi River (1838–39).

Chapter 15

REPAIRING THE
ALTAR OF WORSHIP

WORSHIP IS THE THIRD STRATEGIC INSTRUMENT REQUIRED for dismantling structures. Elijah's repairing the altar was important in overcoming the prophets of Baal and Asherah. The passage is long but important.

> Then Elijah said to all the people, "Come near to me." So all the people came near to him. And he repaired the altar of the LORD which had been torn down. Elijah took twelve stones according to the number of the tribes of the sons of Jacob, to whom the word of the LORD had come, saying, "Israel shall be your name."
>
> So with the stones he built an altar in the name of the LORD, and he made a trench around the altar, large enough to hold two measures of seed. Then he arranged the wood and cut the ox in pieces and laid it on the wood. And he said, "Fill four pitchers with water and pour it on the burnt offering and on the wood." And he said, "Do it a second time," and they

did it a second time. And he said, "Do it a third
time," and they did it a third time. The water flowed
around the altar and he also filled the trench with
water.

At the time of the offering of the evening sacrifice,
Elijah the prophet came near and said, "O Lord, the
God of Abraham, Isaac and Israel, today let it be
known that You are God in Israel and that I am Your
servant and I have done all these things at Your
word. Answer me, O Lord, answer me, that this people may know that You, O Lord, are God, and that
You have turned their heart back again."

Then the fire of the LORD fell and consumed the
burnt offering and the wood and the stones and the
dust, and licked up the water that was in the trench.

When all the people saw it, they fell on their faces;
and they said, "The LORD, He is God; the LORD, He
is God." (1 Kings 18:30-39)

Elijah repaired the altar, prepared the sacrifice, prayed and God
showed up in power. Elijah's act of obedience and worship caused the
people to realize that the Lord was God. The result was more extravagant worship, weakening the Jezebel structure in the nation.

A few years ago on a Sunday morning at our church, The Life
Center in San Antonio, we were in a very deep place of worship. As
we exalted the greatness and majesty of the Lord, His saturating presence descended upon us. While we sang, "Spirit of the Sovereign Lord,
come and make Your presence known, reveal the glory of the risen

Lord. Let the weight of Your glory cover us,"[1] the Lord gave me a vision, which is rare for me. I saw the Lord arrayed in white with gold armor riding on a white horse decked with gold bridle and saddle. The horse was high stepping very, very slowly as we worshipped and invited the Lord's presence, His kingdom rule and His glory. I saw behind the horse the army—walking, robed in white, without armor and weapons—just worshipping and exalting the King of Glory. Then the Lord said to me, "I war in My glory."

> I saw behind the horse the army—walking, robed in white, without armor and weapons—just worshipping and exalting the King of Glory. Then the Lord said to me, "I war in My glory."

God Wars in His Glory

Think about it. We can war. You've probably done it many times by wielding spiritual weapons like the name of Jesus, the blood of Jesus, and the word of the Lord. The Bible talks about *the weapons of our warfare* (2 Corinthians 10:3-5). It's not wrong to war. However, when *God* wars, there is a difference. I want to understand how to worship the Lord in such a way that His glory comes and *He wars*.

When it comes to dismantling structures in political parties and in local government, we need the Lord to war. That will depend upon the quality, intensity, sincerity and even the location of our worship. I've already shared about worship at the Republican State Conventions in 1998, 2000, and 2002. Amazing things happened when we prepared the convention centers with worship and repentance in Fort Worth, Houston, and Dallas. Since then I've seen God move in multiethnic meetings in various venues—especially political events.

When we worship, we speak *to* the Lord Himself in the first person unlike when we praise and speak *about* the Lord's works and character to each other in the third person.

> The Lord reigns: Let the earth rejoice: Let the multi-
> tude of isles be glad! Clouds and darkness surround
> [You]. Righteousness and justice are the foundation
> of [Your] throne. A fire goes before [You], and burns
> up [Your] enemies round about. [Your] lightnings
> light the world. The earth sees and trembles. The
> mountains melt like wax at [Your] presence, [O]
> Lord, at Your presence, Lord of the whole earth. The
> heavens declare [Your] righteousness, and all the
> peoples see [Your] glory."
> (Psalm 97:1-6, parentheses mine)

> Gird Your sword upon Your thigh, O Mighty One,
> with Your glory and Your majesty. And in Your maj-
> esty ride prosperously because of truth, humility and
> righteousness. And Your right hand shall teach You
> awesome things. Your arrows are sharp in the heart
> of the King's enemies. The peoples fall under You.
> (Psalm 45:3–5)

As we worship, *He wars!!!* He dismantles altars of false worship. The light of His glory blinds the eyes of the enemy, and the cloud of His glory confuses the enemy. *He* overcomes as *we* worship. In her book *Glory—Experiencing the Atmosphere of Heaven*, Ruth Ward Heflin admonishes, "Praise ... until the spirit of worship comes. Worship ... until the glory comes. Then ... stand in the glory."[2]

Worship That Brings God's Glory

The worship that brings God's glory is the kind of worship that most believers rarely, if ever, experience. Study worship in the Book of Revelation to understand worship that attracts the glory of God. Welcome the sound of heaven. It is worship *to Him* that extols His majesty, His beauty, His power, His authority, and His glory. It's not personal love songs, as sweet as they are. It's not prophetic songs that extol His greatness to each other. It is full-throttled adoration, exaltation, and magnification that ascribe to the Lord the glory due His name. It's in His glory that He wars.

> In that day the Lord with His severe sword, great
> and strong, will punish Leviathan the fleeing ser-
> pent, Leviathan that twisted serpent, and He will
> slay the reptile that is in the sea. (Isaiah 27:1)

Unholy structures shall not prevail against the King of kings and Lord of lords warring in His glory—enthroned upon the praises of His people, establishing His throne of justice and righteousness and His everlasting kingdom. It's in that place where the increase of His government has no end.

> Unholy structures shall not prevail against the King of kings and Lord of lords warring in His glory.

You have increased the nation, O Lord, You have increased the nation. You are glorified. You have expanded all the borders of the land. (Isaiah 26:15)

You are exalted, O Lord. You are Eternal God. God of Abraham, Isaac and Jacob. Everlasting Father, Creator, Giver of Life. Compassionate One, Forgiving One, Faithful One. Redeemer, Master, Savior. King of kings, Lord of lords, true Lawgiver and Righteous Judge. You are above all gods. You are great and greatly to be praised. You reign in majesty. We welcome Your presence, O God. We welcome Your authority. We welcome Your rule and Your kingdom. Let Your kingdom come. Let all the nations praise You, O God. You are great. You are the God of miracles. We invite You to reign over our lives, over America and over the nations. Take up Your throne, O God, and reign over us. We ascribe to You glory, honor, power, and blessing. There is none like You. Who can stand before You, O Righteous Judge? We open the gates and invite You in. Come in Your power. Come in Your glory. You alone are holy. You alone are worthy. We humble ourselves before You and give You all of the glory.

Now is the time to worship, to humble ourselves in brokenness in His presence. Now is the time to stand in authority to release the word that He puts in our mouths to confront, to pluck up and to pull down. We are worshipping warriors going forth with authority to invite His presence, to repent, to wail, to worship and to take territory. We come in the opposite spirit to dismantle both Jezebel and Ahab structures. Then He can use us "to rebuild the ancient ruins, to raise up the age-old foundations and to repair the breach" (Isaiah 58:12) so that the kingdom of God will be established on the earth. Go in early and worship in your office, on your school campus, wherever you are. Exalt the Lord and give Him the first and highest place in your sphere of influence. Just as I experienced in the political arena, He will come into Your sphere when You give Him access through worship.

> Exalt the Lord and give Him the first and highest place in your sphere of influence. He will come into Your sphere when You give Him access through worship.

We must rise up in the spirit of Elijah to dismantle structures imbedded in both political parties. It's God who reigns, not a political party.

ON THE GOVERNMENTAL GRASSROOTS LEVEL

When I was Field Director for TXCC, we took over the Republican Party of Texas. In 1992, the TXCC Chairman invited the head of a pro-life organization, an Eagle Forum leader, and me to a meeting in his office. All of us had been engaged in the Republican Party platform battle for years to insure that the party platform supported the social issues of the day: sanctity of human life, religious liberty, traditional marriage, and other Judeo-Christian values. Each had a network of people on their mailing lists who were interested in moral values. The chairman wanted to take over the Republican Party of Texas organization—the chairman, vice-chairman, SREC (State Republican Executive Committee), and national committeeman and committeewoman. What did we think about it? Everyone agreed. The chairman had the delegate numbers from every senatorial district printed out for us. He gave them to me, and I started organizing TXCC county chapters based on the delegate-strength numbers by state senatorial districts.

Network for Victory

When I organized a county chapter, I sent the contact information to approximately 10 pro-family leaders we were in alliance with. It was a cooperative effort. Pro-family leaders had organized in the Dallas/ Fort Worth Metroplex and the Greater Houston area. Those two areas had the most delegates because of population. Already a large number of pro-life activists attended the Republican State Convention from those two areas. Many smaller counties had never even had a Republican Primary Election, so there had been no delegates from those counties.

I know it's hard to believe, but Texas was a Democratic state. Democratic Governor Ann Richards headed up the executive branch and Democrats controlled both the House and the Senate in the Texas Legislature. I began to organize chapters all over the state with priorities on counties that had significant population numbers. I connected the leaders we recruited to other chapter leaders in their state senatorial district because that's the way the state convention was organized.

> We had taken over the Republican Party structure because we knew the rules, had a plan, and engaged a lot of people in the process.

By the June 1992 convention, we had a majority of pro-life delegates at the convention and were able to elect a few SREC members. However, we had never been *inside* before so we didn't know the rules. Prior to 1992, less than 10 of the 62 people on the SREC were pro-life. In 1994 we elected the chairman, vice-chairman, and over 50 percent of the SREC. By June of 1996, 66 percent of the SREC were pro-life as well as the chairman, vice chairman, national committeeman, and national committeewoman. We had taken over the Republican Party structure because we knew the rules, had a plan, and engaged a lot of people in the process.

Let me be clear about this. We were not *welcomed* into the Republican Party on the county level, the senatorial district level, the state level, or the national level. People who are in power don't want to give it up, even if they share your values. The Republican Party platform had been pro-life since 1976, the first presidential election year after Roe v. Wade was decided in 1973. Social conservatives engaged in the Republican Party process in great numbers when Ronald Reagan first ran for office, although a few had gotten involved in the early 1960s.

The Texas Republican Party platform was excellent on less taxes, the sanctity of life, marriage, and religious liberty. Even though a few of the people who ran the Republican Party of Texas were social as well as fiscal conservatives, their faith was not the motivating factor that it was for the new Republicans. For the most part, social conservative activists were focused on the platform and had never considered taking over the structure of this political party. But an alliance of pro-family organizations did take it over. Although TXCC no longer exists, religious conservatives still run the Republican Party of Texas. Sadly, they are not as active in racial issues as they were when Susan was chairman, but they are still encouraging grassroots activists to be involved.

White Christians have been engaged in the political party process for years, but only a few Black and Hispanic Christians are engaged.

America Is Waiting

America is waiting for godly believers of every ethnicity to engage in the process. It is not a matter of which political party you choose. The point is to engage your faith and values in the process. Make a difference for your generation and those to come. If you consider yourself a Democrat, engage in the process as an individual and plan to lead a national campaign to mobilize believers who consider themselves to be Democrats to change the stated values of the Democratic Party and weaken the unholy structure behind it.

> America is waiting for godly believers of every ethnicity to engage in the process. It is not a matter of which political party you choose. The point is to engage your faith and values in the process. Make a difference for your generation and those to come.

If you have a national network and want to have a seat at the table, don't wait for someone to invite you in. It will never happen. You must educate a number of believers in every state to engage in the process. Brace yourself and prepare for a battle. Even people who agree with you on the issues will be suspicious. Don't let that stop you. Show up. Engage in the process beginning on the local, grassroots level. Go in with a smile on your face. Introduce yourself. Find a place to serve. Be prepared to stand. Bring others into the process on the local level for *the long haul*.

Think how many years it took to get Civil Rights legislation passed in our nation after the Reconstruction legislation was repealed.

Almost 100 years! This will not happen overnight. However, if you continue to show up, invite others into the process, and finally lay out a plan with key people in each state to educate and mobilize values votes, it can happen. If you are serious, have a network, and are aligned with biblical values, I am available to help you, no matter which political party you are in. My contact information is in the About the Author section at the back of this book.

If you want to see America changed, apply the principles in this book and begin to organize on the grassroots level. In addition, give this book to key leaders that you know in the Black and Hispanic community. Build a multiracial coalition including Asian Americans, Native Americans, and others and move forward. America is waiting for you.

I've asked you to pray with me throughout this book, now let me pray for you.

> *Dear Father, thank you for Your grace on the reader to*
> *finish this book. I pray for the Person of Color reading*
> *these words. Thank You for setting him/her free to move*
> *forward. Lord, I see individuals of every culture liberated*
> *by the truth and by Your Spirit to step out of deception*
> *and engage. Father, I see leaders who can mobilize, have*
> *networks and are gifted in organizing. Lord, I ask for Your*
> *anointing to break every yoke of bondage. I release him/her*
> *to move higher, to go further, and to turn this country*
> *around by engaging believers of every ethnicity to take*
> *their place at the decision-making table. Some will not*
> *only take a place at the table, but also will engage with*
> *others to **own the table**. Lord, I pray for alignment with*

believers already in the process. Let there be a multiracial alliance to engage the Body of Christ and position it for victory in the political arena. I release courage. I release anointing. I release a burning desire to see America led by godly men and women full of wisdom and integrity. I release a convening anointing. I release a mantle for reconciliation, humility, and worship. I release a call to the wailing women to come together and cry out. May the kingdoms of this world become the kingdoms of our Lord and of His Christ and may we be positioned to reign with Him in our local, state, and federal government. May our loyalty be to the Lord Jesus Christ and may a movement of values voters led by Black and Hispanic Americans sweep this nation—in Jesus' Name.

Now is your time. Rise up, move forward and engage. Engage is the operative word. Engage in prayer. Engage in worship. Engage in Bible study. Engage in civic action. Engage in every election. Engage in a political party. Make your voice heard and your influence known. If you have enough people with you, you can even change the system—from systemic racism, systemic poverty, and systemic hopelessness to systemic righteousness and systemic justice. America awaits.

---

[1] Andy Park, "Spirit of the Sovereign Lord," (Bentley, WA: Mercy, Vineyard Publishing, 1994).

[2] Ruth Ward Heflin, *Glory—Experiencing the Atmosphere of Heaven*, (Hagerstown, MD: The McDougal Publishing Company, 1990), xii.

Appendix A

A COVENANT WITH LIFE: RECLAIMING MLK'S LEGACY

By Dr. Alveda C. King, *The Black Republican*, www.nbra.info, Fall/Winter 2008-2009.

America has entered into a covenant or a culture of death. May God have mercy, and restore us to a covenant of life!

Isaiah 28:15 - Because ye have said, We have made a covenant with death, and with hell are we at agreement; when the overflowing scourge shall pass through, it shall not come unto us: for we have made lies our refuge, and under falsehood have we hid ourselves:

Isaiah 28:18 - And your covenant with death shall be disannulled, and your agreement with hell shall not stand; when the overflowing scourge shall pass through, then ye shall be trodden down by it.

• • • • • • • • • • •

As a Christian Civil Rights Activist, I can remember a time in America when black people looked to God for answers. This recollection brings to mind a startling revelation: God is not a Democrat, nor a Republican! In light of the emergence of a black man as a presidential contender this election season, we might do well to take note that it is not the political party or the man, but the message that is imperative.

In his "I Have a Dream" speech, my uncle, Dr. Martin Luther King, Jr., said: "I have a dream that my four children will one day live in a nation where they will not be judged by the color of their skin, but by the content of their character."

Today, as enlightened, informed African-Americans living in America, we must demand that candidates represent our views — and always vote your values!

As a Republican, my goal is always to seek the will of God for good government, and then to demand accountability from all elected leaders. We are off track, seeking solutions from government, when we should be seeking the grace of God!

A brief history lesson can reveal how we got to a place of looking to man instead of God for answers.

In 1960, Senator John F. Kennedy defeated sitting Vice President Richard Nixon in the bid to become president. The black vote swung the tide!

My grandfather, Dr. Martin Luther King, Sr., or "Daddy King", was a Republican and father of Dr. Martin Luther King, Jr. who was a Republican.

Daddy King influenced a reported 100,000 black voters to cast previously Republican votes for Senator Kennedy even though Kennedy had voted against the 1957 Civil Rights Law. Mrs. King had appealed to Kennedy and Nixon to help her husband, and Nixon who had voted for the 1957 Civil Rights Law did not respond. At the urging of his advisors, Kennedy made a politically calculated phone call to Mrs. King, who was pregnant at the time, bringing the attention of the nation to Dr. King's plight.

Moved by Mrs. King's gratitude for Senator Kennedy's intervention, Daddy King was very grateful to Senator Kennedy for his assistance in rescuing Dr. King, Jr. from a life threatening jail encounter. This experience led to a black exodus from the Republican Party.

Thus, this one simple act of gratitude caused black America to quickly forget that the Republican Party was birthed in America as the antislavery party to end the scourge of slavery and combat the terror of racism and segregation. They quickly forgot that the Democratic Party was the party of the Ku Klux Klan.

Banished from memory was the fact that the Democratic Party fought to keep blacks in slavery and in 1894 overturned the civil rights laws of the 1860's that had been passed by Republicans, after the Republicans also amended the Constitution to grant blacks freedom, citizenship and the right to vote.

Forgotten was the fact that it was the Republicans who started the HBCUs [Historically Black Colleges and Universities] and the NAACP [National Association for the Advancement of Colored People] to stop the Democrats from lynching blacks. Into the dust bin of history was tossed the fact that it was the Republicans led by Republican Senator Everett Dirksen who pushed to pass the civil rights laws in 1957, 1960, 1964, 1965 and 1968.

Removed from memory are the facts that it was Republican President Dwight Eisenhower who sent troops to Arkansas to desegregate schools, established the Civil Rights Commission in 1958, and appointed Chief Justice Early Warren to the U.S. Supreme Court which resulted in the 1954 *Brown v. Board of Education* decision ending school segregation.

Meanwhile Democrats in Congress were still fighting to prevent the passage of new civil rights laws that would overturn those discriminatory Black Codes and Jim Crow laws that had been enacted by Democrats in the South. There would have been no law for President Lyndon Johnson to sign in 1964 had it not been for the Republicans breaking the Democrats' filibuster of the law and pushing to have that landmark legislation enacted.

No one batted an eye when President Kennedy opposed the 1963 March on Washington by Dr. King. Hardly a ripple of protest was uttered when President Kennedy, through his brother Attorney General Robert Kennedy, had Dr. King wiretapped and investigated on suspicion of being a Communist.

Little attention was paid to the fact that it was a Democrat, Public Safety Commissioner Eugene "Bull" Conner, who in 1963 turned dogs and fire hoses on Dr. King and other civil rights protestors. No one noted that it was a Democrat, Georgia Governor Lester Maddox, who waved ax handles to stop blacks from patronizing his restaurant. Nor was heed paid to the fact that it was a Democrat, Alabama Governor George Wallace, who stood in front of the Alabama schoolhouse in 1963 and thundered: "Segregation now, segregation tomorrow, segregation forever." None of those racist Democrats became Republicans.

During this time of turmoil, completely forgotten was the fact that it was Democrat Arkansas Governor Orville Faubus who in 1954 had blocked desegregation of a Little Rock public school. To their eternal shame, the chief opponents of the landmark 1964 Civil Rights Act were Democrats Senators Sam Ervin, Albert Gore, Sr. and Robert Byrd, a former Klansman [and sitting United States Senator today]. All of the racist Democrats that Dr. King was fighting remained Democrats until the day they died. How can anyone today think that Dr. King, my uncle, would have joined the party of the KKK?

There is a law of unexpected outcomes. Who could have predicted that the black exodus from the Republican Party to the Democratic Party in the 1960's would have also ushered in decades of destruction which continue to plague our communities today? So what happened during those ensuring decades? Let's review the saga that continues.

In June of 1963, the Supreme Court upheld the argument of the atheist, Madelyn Murray O'Hair, and granted her petition — a decision whose profound and oppressive influence worked to ensure that God was evicted from public society, across the entire spectrum of the American governmental system. From that day to this, not only has prayer been outlawed, God's very name has also been declared anathema to the United States Constitution — forbidden to be mentioned in any federal, state, county, city or municipal context.

As a legacy of O'Hair's dark, anti-God plan, other edicts emerged. Not only is prayer forbidden in the public forum, but prohibited also is the spiritually uplifting display of the cross. The Ten Commandments are forbidden. The Bible is forbidden. Nativity plays are forbidden. Even the mere mention of the name of "God" or "Jesus" in schools is forbidden. More far reaching and sinister than that, anything that is even suggestive of those names is forbidden.

Ten years after O'Hair's dark victory, another unholy bargain with the covenant of death arose — the *Roe v. Wade* decision in the US Supreme Court which enabled the scourges of hell to kill our children. The Democratic Party, including their most recently celebrated presidential nominee gives blanket support to upholding *Roe v. Wade*, along with support for a $300+ million a year federal tax grant to Planned Parenthood, America's largest abortion provider. Planned Parenthood was founded by racist eugenicist Margaret Sanger.

Bereft of the choice to read the Bible and pray in schools, and armed with the power to abort babies, our children and youth are dealing with a double portion of O'Hare's covenant of death legacy. A sea of innocent blood is being spilled across our country and around the world. Children are being preyed upon and murdered by depraved adults who should be their protectors.

While the debate over whether God's name should be outlawed from our society, and whether abortion and infanticide should be condoned, a voice in the wilderness continues to cry out, "what about the children?" That voice is being drowned out by the raucous noise of the anti-God secularists and pro-abortion advocates.

Who can hear the voices of thousands of children who are terrorized in the halls and classrooms of their schools? Who can hear the silent cry of each baby who is artificially breached before coming to term in his or her mother's womb, only to have her skull punctured, and feel, yes agonizingly "feel", the life run out of her before she takes her first breath of freedom? Who among us is so cold-blooded as to vote to deny health care to a baby born alive during a late-term abortion and allow that baby to die? There is a crisis in our community of our own making. The abortion rate in black communities is three times that of whites and twice that of Hispanics, according to the Guttmacher Institute, a reproductive health research group.

Yes, we must be concerned about health care benefits, affordable housing, adequate food, jobs and justice. We must also be concerned about the higher God-inspired principles of life, liberty and the pursuit of happiness — principles that are enshrined in our nation's founding document, the US Constitution.

In this great country of ours, no one should be forced to pray or read any religious documents, and a woman should have the right to decide what to do with her own body. Thank God for the Constitution. That Constitution, though, guarantees freedom *of* religion, not freedom *from* religion. The so-called doctrine of "separation of church and state" is not in our Constitution. Nothing in our constitution forbids the free exercise of religion in the public square. Inherent in our Constitutional right to life, liberty and the pursuit of happiness, is the right to know the serious consequences of making a decision to deny religious freedom, or to abort our children.

Oh, God, what would Martin Luther King, Jr., who dreamed of having his four children judged by the content of their characters, not just the color of their skin, do if he'd lived to see the contents of thousands of children's skulls emptied into the bottomless caverns of the abortionists pits? What would he say about the rivers of blood of the children cut down in gang wars and other dark deeds?

It is time for America, perhaps the most blessed nation on earth, to lead the world in repentance, and in restoration of life! If only we can carry the freedom of repentance to its fullest potential. If only America can repent and turn away from the sins of our nation. We must allow light and life back into our lives!

Today, I live with a repentant, heavy heart, and I pray each day for the Lord's forgiveness and blessing. I am a mother of six living children and a grandmother. Regretfully, I am also a post-abortive mother. I offer a tearful prayer that my sharing the tragedy of my life-altering experiences will help save the life of a child yet unborn. In the early 1970's, I suffered one involuntary and one voluntary "legal" abortion.

My involuntary abortion was performed just prior to *Roe v .Wade* by my private pro-abortion physician without my consent. I had gone to the doctor to ask why my cycle had not resumed after the birth of my son. I did not ask for and did not want an abortion. The doctor said, "You don't need to be pregnant, let's see." He proceeded to perform a painful examination which resulted in a gush of blood and tissue emanating from my womb. He explained that he had performed an abortion called a "local D and C."

Soon after the *Roe v. Wade* decision, I became pregnant again. There was adverse pressure and threat of violence from the baby's father. The ease and convenience provided through *Roe v. Wade* made it too easy for me to make the fateful and fatal decision to abort our child.

I went to a Planned Parenthood sanctioned doctor and was advised that the procedure would hurt no more than "having a tooth removed." The next day, I was admitted to the hospital, and our baby was aborted. My medical insurance paid for the procedure. As soon as I woke up, I knew that something was very wrong. I felt very ill, and very empty. I tried to talk to the doctor and nurses about it. They assured me that "it will all go away in a few days. You will be fine." They lied.

Over the next few years, I experienced medical problems. I had trouble bonding with my son, and his five siblings who were born after the abortions. I began to suffer from eating disorders, depression, nightmares, sexual dysfunctions and a host of other issues related to the abortion that I chose to have. I felt angry about both the involuntary and voluntary abortions, and very guilty about the abortion I chose to have. The guilt made me very ill. Like my uncle, Dr. Martin Luther King, Jr. who had received the Margaret Sanger Planned Parenthood Award in 1968, I became a victim to the lies of Planned Parenthood. They told my uncle, they told me and millions of mothers and fathers that their agenda was to help our people. They lied. Their agenda is deadly!

I pray often for deliverance from the pain caused by my decision to abort my baby. I suffered the threat of cervical and breast cancer, and experienced the pain of empty arms after the baby was gone. Truly, for me, and countless abortive mothers, nothing on earth can fully restore what has been lost — only Jesus can.

My children have all suffered from knowing that they have a brother or sister that their mother chose to abort. Often they ask if I ever thought about aborting them, and they have said, "You killed our baby." This is very painful for all of us. My mother and grandparents were very sad to know about the loss of the baby. The aborted child's father also regrets the abortion. If it had not been for *Roe v. Wade*, I would never have had that abortion.

My birthday is January 22, and each year this special day is marred by the fact that it is also the anniversary of *Roe v. Wade* — and the anniversary of death for millions of babies. I and my deceased children are victims of abortion. The *Roe v. Wade* decision has adversely affected the lives of my entire family.

My grandfather, Dr. Martin Luther King, Sr., twice said, "No one is going to kill a child of mine." The first time Daddy King said this was to my mother, who was facing an "inconvenient pregnancy" with me. The next time, I was facing a pregnancy, and told him about it. In both instances, Daddy King said no, and saved his seed.

Tragically, two of his grandchildren had already been aborted when he saved the life of his next great-grandson with this statement. His son, Dr. Martin Luther King, Jr., once said, "The Negro cannot win as long as he is willing to sacrifice the lives of his children for comfort and safety." How can the "Dream" survive if we murder our children? Every aborted baby is like a slave in the womb of his or her mother. In the hands of the mother is the fate of that child — whether the child lives or dies — a decision given to the mother by *Roe v. Wade*. That choice, the final choice of whether the child lives or dies, should be left to God, Who ultimately says "choose life!"

I join the voices of thousands across America, who are SILENT NO MORE. We can no longer sit idly by and allow this horrible spirit of murder to cut down, yes cut out and cut away, our unborn and destroy the lives of our mothers. I am very grateful to God for the Spirit of Repentance that is sweeping our land. In repentance there is healing. In the name of Jesus, we must humble ourselves and pray, and turn from our wicked ways, so that God will hear from Heaven and Heal Our Land.

I, like my uncle, Martin Luther King, Jr., have a dream. I have a dream that someday the men and women of our nation, the boys and girls of America will come to our senses, humble ourselves before God Almighty and receive His healing grace. I pray that this is the day and the hour of our deliverance. I pray that we will regain a covenant of life and finally obtain the promised liberty, justice and pursuit of happiness for all. Let us end injustice anywhere by championing justice everywhere, including in the womb.

• • • • • • • • • • •

May God, by His grace, have mercy on us all.

PASTORAL ASSOCIATE, PRIESTS FOR LIFE, DR. ALVEDA C. KING founded King for America, Inc. "to assist people in enriching their lives spiritually, personally, mentally and economically." She is the daughter of the late slain civil rights activist Rev. A. D. King and his wife Naomi Barber King. Alveda is the grateful mother of six children and she is a doting grandmother.

During the more than half century of her life, Alveda has worked towards her purpose of glorifying God in the earth by accomplishing many goals. Currently, Alveda is a minister of the Gospel of Jesus Christ, serving as Director of African American Outreach for Gospel of Life, headed up by Father Frank Pavone of Priests for Life. She also consults with the Africa Humanitarian Christian Fellowship, founded by her mentor, Pastor Allen McNair of Believers' Bible Christian Church in Atlanta, Georgia.

She is a former college professor, holding the Masters of Arts degree in Business Management from Central Michigan University. Her undergraduate studies in journalism and sociology helped her to become a published author, the most popular works being her best selling books Sons of Thunder: The King Family Legacy, and I Don't Want Your Man, I Want My Own. This inspirational collection of Christian testimonies is used at conferences and workshops around the world.

Alveda's Doctorate of Laws was conferred by Saint Anslem College. She has served on the boards and committees of numerous organizations Coalition of African American Pastors, and the Judeo-Christian Coalition for Constitutional Restoration. She also served in the Georgia State House of Representatives, and is an accomplished actress and songwriter. She is a voice for the Silent No More Awareness Campaign, speaking about her regret for her abortion.

During the years of the Civil Rights Movement, led by her Uncle, Dr. Martin Luther King, Jr., Alveda's family home was bombed in Birmingham, Alabama in the heat of the struggle. "Daddy's house was bombed, then in Louisville, Kentucky his church office was bombed. I was also jailed during the open housing movement," she recalls.

Alveda has continued her long-term work as a civil rights activist, speaking out on issues that face society today. "I believe that School Choice is a pressing civil rights issue. Perhaps the most compelling issue of all is the life of the unborn," Alveda says. "Faith in God, and the commitment to fulfill His will for our lives -- not faith in government bureaucracy - is the key to positive action. Have faith in God!" This is the message that Alveda carries to the world.

To arrange a media interview, contact Jerry Horn at (540) 785-4733, Email: media@priestsforlife.org To invite Alveda King to speak in your area, contact our Travel Department at 888-PFL-3448, ext. 255; Fax: 718-980-7191; Email: travels@priestsforlife.org.

Appendix B

THE PRICE IS RIGHT? PAYOFFS FOR SENATORS TYPICAL IN HEALTH CARE BILL

FOXNews.com

Monday: Sen. Ben Nelson talks to reporters on Capitol Hill. (AP Photo)

Sen. Ben Nelson's hardly the only lawmaker extracting sweetheart deals out of the health care reform bill.

While the Nebraska Democrat got a particularly juicy concession in exchange for a "yes" vote on the 10-year, $871 billion package—permanent and full federal aid for his state's expanded Medicaid population—support from a slew of other senators likewise came with a price.

Western states got more money for hospitals that serve Medicare patients. Louisiana got up to $300 million in Medicaid benefits. The list goes on.

Senate Republicans lined up Saturday to decry the latest deal targeted toward Nebraska, which was decried as the "cornhusker kickback."

"Votes have been bought," Sen. Saxby Chambliss, R-Ga., said.

But Senate Democrats said the payoffs are nothing unusual, and in fact typical.

"People fight for their own states. That's the nature of a democracy," Sen. Amy Klobuchar, D-Minn., said on "Fox News Sunday," defending Nelson against withering attacks from the GOP.

"This is just part of the normal legislative process," said Jim Manley, spokesman for Senate Majority Leader Harry Reid.

As a measure of just how typical they are, a slew of payoffs and concessions have been struck over the past several months.

- Sen. Mary Landrieu, D-La., won between $100 million and $300 million in additional federal aid for her state's Medicaid population. The deal, secured before she cast her critical vote in favor of bringing the health bill to the floor, was immediately dubbed the "Louisiana Purchase," though the actual Louisiana Purchase was considerably cheaper.

- Vermont and Massachusetts got $1.2 billion in Medicaid money—change that was described as a correction to the current system which exempts those two states because they have robust health care systems. Vermont Sen. Bernie Sanders also boasted Saturday that he requested and won an investment worth between $10 and $14 billion for community health centers.

- Western states secured higher federal reimbursement rates for doctors and hospitals that serve Medicare patients. The provision covers the low-population "frontier" states and applies to Montana, North Dakota, South Dakota, Utah and Wyoming -- the latter two states are both represented by two Republicans, but ended up as beneficiaries anyway since they qualify. The legislative language defines frontier states as states where at least 50 percent of the counties have fewer than six people per square mile. Sen. Kent Conrad, D-N.D., chairman of the Senate Budget Committee, defended the "special deal," telling "Fox News Sunday" that those five states were getting an increase in reimbursements because they get the lowest amount in the country. "That doesn't offend me at all," he said. "It's in fact, fair."

- Florida, New York and Pennsylvania—here five of six senators are Democrats—will have their seniors' Medicare Advantage benefits protected, even as the program sees massive cuts elsewhere.

- Sen. Max Baucus, D-Mont., reportedly secured expanded Medicare coverage for victims of asbestos exposure in a mine in Libby, Mont.

- Connecticut is receiving $100 million for a "health care facility" affiliated with an academic health center at a university that contains the state's only "public academic medical and dental school."

- Nebraska's Nelson won permanent federal aid for his state's expanded Medicaid population, a benefit worth up to $100 million over 10 years. Other states get the federal aid for three years, but Nebraska's benefit is indefinite. His state also got an exemption for nonprofit insurance companies from a health insurance company tax. Many believe this was targeted at Mutual of Omaha, but senior Democratic aides would not confirm that.

Independent Sen. Joe Lieberman didn't extract any payoffs for Connecticut. Rather, he succeeded in stripping the government-run insurance plan from the Senate health bill, along with a proposed expansion of Medicare that he recently said he opposes.

Fox News' Trish Turner contributed to this report, December 21, 2009

http://www.foxnews.com/politics/2009/12/21/price-right-payoffs-senators-typical-health-care

ACKNOWLEDGMENTS

H{ow can I thank everyone} who has encouraged me, taught me, and prayed me through this book? It would take another book!

First of all, thank you, **John**, for praying for me, encouraging me, and nudging me to keep at it until the book was completed. You have served me, cared for me, and inspired me. Although you are my primary intercessor, as well as my husband, there are many more who prayed for me. **Falma Rufus**. Thank you for the tears you shed, **Falma**, while reading the manuscript through for "race sensitivity." You were my first indication that what I had written would do what I prayed it would. Thank you for taking it to your intercessors and for praying it through. Thank you, intercessors, for being faithful to carry this book and to send me notes along the way: **Lee Noack, Lucille Ellison, Leslie Ellison, Nancy Mitchell, Hank and Marilyn Marion, David Gatti, Hollis and Carol Jean Kirkpatrick, Mary Ann Tittsworth, Brenda Callahan, Guilda Bueno, Rini Roach, Nita Lopez, Carlos and Thelma Rendon, Gene and Sylvia Juarez, Rudy Davila, Jr.,** and **Kathleen Withers**. Thanks to all of you who read the manuscript and gave constructive ways to improve it.

Thank you, **Norma Anderson, Linda Fletcher**, and **Cathe Halford** for help with editing. Norma, your masterful touch greatly improved the finished product. Cathe, you were there in the beginning—walking through much of the story and encouraging me in walking it out as well as in writing.

Thank you, **Kyle Duncan**, for being there at just the right time with wisdom and direction.

Thank you, **David Sluka**, for the internal design and engineering the process through to completion. You are a joy to work with. Your creativity and sensitivity along with the cover designer, **Steve Fryer**, made a potentially stressful process a journey of grace. I love your ideas and your speedy execution. Steve, your cover is beautiful. You are a great, anointed team.

Thank you, **Cindy Oliveira**, for a last-minute proofread and administrating all the pieces of the publishing process. When you called to say that Ed wanted to put the book on the fast track, you meant it. Thank you for your continuing grace and excellence. You are beautiful.

Thank you, **Dave Thompson**, for taking time to read the book and comment on every aspect of the process. Your insight and encouragement gave much-needed and appreciated perspective. Thank you for your wisdom and encouragement at just the right times in living out portions of my journey.

Thank you, Pastor **Jeff Mullen** of Point of Grace in Waukee, Iowa, for your recommendation and call to **Becki Ramsey** of Out of the Ashes Photography to request a quick photo job. Thank you, Becki, for giving me your time and wonderful, finished product. You take great "senior pictures."

Thank you, **Gay Thurman**, for your friendship and inspiration. You and Cathe were there at the beginning, and you're still on the Lord's path.

To my spiritual father, **Ed Silvoso**, I am deeply grateful for your example and inspiration. In your busy schedule you found time for me. You have opened many doors for me, and this book is by far the largest. Thank you.

Dr. **C. Peter Wagner**, when you called after having read the book and told me you liked it, my heart soared. You gave me your valuable time to counsel me. What a gift you are.

Thank you, Dr. **Shirley Clark**, for your heart for our nation, for your leadership in the area of strategic prayer, unity and reconciliation, and for endorsing me. You excel at so many things, not the least of which is keeping relationships. There is more for us to do together.

I appreciate my special friends who took the time to read my book and to endorse it. Your words and your lives have impacted me and I am grateful to you. Apostle **Willie F. Wooten** from New Orleans, your friendship and leadership are dear to me. I honor and appreciate you. Thank you, Dr. **Jay Swallow**, for all you've done to heal the land of America. There is more for you to do and much more for all of us to learn from you. Thank you for your leadership and your endorsement. **Merrie Cardin**, you have prayed for me, encouraged me, and given me a platform. You have helped to carry me through this process. Thank you for your endorsement and so much more. **Karen Harris**, such a beautiful person and wise counselor. Thank you for your wisdom and encouragement. Yes, God's *chronos* (chronological time) connected with His *kairos* (opportune time) for this book. Thank you, **Laurraine Huffman**, for pioneering racial reconciliation and transformation in El Paso, and for your prayers, support, and precise endorsement. You are wonderful. I appreciate you, **Will Ford III**, for understanding the times, sharing your insight with me, for praying and speaking into our nation, and for what you mean to me. Thank you for your endorsement. Thank you, Pastor **Mark Gonzales**, for your sacrificial leadership across the nation, for your friendship and your endorsement. May the Lord continue to give you His favor as you educate and mobilize Hispanics across the nation. Thank you, **Hollis Kirkpatrick**, for the attention you gave to this manuscript and the entire process. Thank you and **C.J.**, for carrying John and me at key times. And thank you for the endorsement. Thank you, Dr. **Melvin D. Johnson**, for your amazing leadership in the political arena over the years as well as from the pulpit. You are a pioneer in what I'm advocating. Your endorsement is appreciated.

Thank you, Dr. **Dell Sanchez**, for being there in the beginning of my journey into America's pain. You spoke into the situation at that time and into my life on many subsequent occasions. Thank you for inviting us to San Antonio ten years ago, for your friendship, and for endorsing this book.

Thank you, Dr. **Tom Schlueter**, for your heart for the nation and for what you've done in strategic prayer and reconciliation in Texas, especially with the Comanche Nation. I appreciate your leadership and your endorsement.

Thank you, **Natalie Hardy**, for your wisdom and honesty. I can always count on you for the truth. Thank you, **Cindy Jacobs**, for encouraging me during the early process of the book. Thank you, **Eddie Smith**, for your writing seminar and for taking time with me on the phone. Thank you, **José Gonzalez**, for reading the manuscript and for the conversation following. Your iron always sharpens mine.

Thank you, **Rune and Berta Brannstrom**, for encouraging John and me, for praying with us and for your leadership in San Antonio.

Thank you, Pastor **Charles and Beverly Burchett**, for walking with us for so many years. You are there on some of the pages of this book, and you are still in our lives today. Thank you for pioneering strategic prayer and racial reconciliation in the hard ground of Deep East Texas, Jasper County.

Thank you, **David and Cheryl Barton**. David, this book could not have been written without your research into hidden Black history as well as America's spiritual heritage. You not only gave me permission to use your material, you thanked me for doing it. You and Cheryl are American treasures. And you, Cheryl, are a seasoned intercessor, always standing in the gap for elected officials and leaders who have found a safe place to share their needs. Thank you for your prayers, encouragement and all you both do for our nation.

Thank you, **special couple**, for funding this book. You have ministered to us in prayer, encouragement, and finances at significant times and ways in our lives. I am deeply grateful. You listen to the Lord and quickly obey. You made the last part of this process easy because of your gift. I pray that the impact of this book in individual lives will be charged to your heavenly accounts.

Thank you, Pastors **Ruben and Lamar Duarte**, for walking through this process as pastors of our church, The Life Center Christian Fellowship in San Antonio, Texas, and as dear friends. How could John and I make this journey without you? When I have important decisions, you are there with wisdom. And many times with just the right words to lift me out of discouragement. I treasure you.

And thank you, **J. D. and Alisa**, **Chad and Marcelle**, **John**, **Kaitlyn**, **Kensley**, **Kaleb**, and **Taryn**—our family—sons, daughters-in-law and grandchildren—for your unconditional love at all times in every way. You are the joy of my life.

ABOUT THE AUTHOR

ALICE PATTERSON, FOUNDER AND PRESIDENT of Justice at the Gate in San Antonio, Texas, is dedicated to empowering believers through reconciliation and education in God's presence to impact our nation through prayer and through the power of the ballot. Alice has been involved in the civic arena since 1984 as President of Permian Basin Eagle Forum, Field Director for Texas Christian Coalition and in various political campaigns. In 1996 she founded Pray Texas to encourage pastors to pray and work together for community transformation. She served as the Texas Coordinator for the United States Strategic Prayer Network for 6 years and served on the U. S. Civil Rights Commission State Advisory Committee for 10 years.

Alice has been described as a "divine connector." She brings pastors and leaders together across denominational, racial and social lines. As the granddaughter of a Ku Klux Klan member, Alice has publicly repented for overt and unconscious racism in the white community. She is working to undo the harm done by her grandfather and others like him. Alice serves as a bridge between Christians of various cultures as well as between the church and the civic arena. Alice oversaw county organization where each of the 254 counties in Texas had a pastor connecting with others in the area for voter registration and voter guide distribution for the November 2005 marriage amendment election.

She has since worked in states like Virginia and Iowa to do the same thing. She convened a group of Hispanic leaders to pray and strategize together to form a national Hispanic organization, which led to a meeting of over 700 Hispanic pastors and spouses in Austin with the Governor of Texas. She hosted a summit of 300 African American Pastors and Leaders to meet with the Governor and other elected officials about the plight of Black children in inner city schools. Alice's heart is to train pastors and leaders in various ethnic communities about how to access governmental power by taking a seat at the decision-making table regardless of political party.

Alice Patterson
Justice at the Gate
PO Box 681148, San Antonio, TX 78268
www.justiceatthegate.org
Tel. 210-677-8214

Other Books from
Transformational Publications

Also Available from Ed Silvoso

Transformation
Change the Marketplace
and You Change the World

Anointed for Business
How to Use Your Influence in the
Marketplace to Change the World

Women: God's Secret Weapon
God's Inspiring Message to Women
of Power, Purpose and Destiny

Prayer Evangelism
How to Change the Spiritual Climate
Over Your Home, Neighborhood and City

That None Should Perish
How to Reach Entire Cities For
Christ Through Prayer Evangelism

Visit our websites to acquire these and other titles.
www.harvestevan.org | www.transformourworld.org
1-800-835-7979

P.O. Box 20310 • San Jose, CA 95160-0310
Tel 408.927.9052 • Fax 408-927-9830 • info@harvestevan.org

Additional Works by Ed Silvoso

TRANSFORMATION IN THE MARKETPLACE *DVD Series*

This DVD series presents riveting true stories of how God is transforming businesses, schools, churches, government, legal and prison systems, cities, states, and a continent, PLUS each DVD includes a step-by-step "how-to" teaching section by Ed Silvoso with powerful insights on how to apply it in your sphere of influence. Titles currently available:

- Olmos Prison, Elk River Story, Transformation Hawaii, The Power of One (four stories on one DVD)
- Transformational Churches
- Transformation in Government and Elected Officials
- Transformation in Youth
- Transformation in Sentul City and Jakarta
- Transformation in Jacksonville, Florida
- Transformation in Paranaque City and Philippines
- Transformation in El Cereso Prison, Mexico
- Transformation in Witbank, South Africa
- Transformation in Uganda

And other New Titles!!

VICTORY AT HOME *Audio Series*

A dynamic, insightful series by Ed Silvoso designed to help couples rediscover intimacy and learn how to prepare children for adolescence with Kingdom values. Rich in biblical and practical insights, this is an ideal tool to restore families to God's intended fullness. *Now availabile on CD!*

BECOMING AN OVERCOMER *Audio Series*

In this powerful series, Ed Silvoso shows how to identify and dismantle spiritual strongholds. Ed defines a stronghold as *a mindset impregnated with hopelessness that forces us to accept as unchangeable situations that we know are contrary to the will of God.* A session on how to forgive the unforgivable is also included. *Now available on CD!*

Visit the Harvest Evangelism website to acquire these and other titles, to learn about upcoming training trips, and to access a variety of practical "how-to" tools by Ed Silvoso and the Harvest Evangelism team.

www.harvestevan.org
1.800.835.7979

HARVEST
EVANGELISM

and
NEW Transformation Website
www.transformourworld.org

P.O. Box 20310 • San Jose, CA 95160-0310
Tel 408.927.9052 • Fax 408.927.9830 • info@harvestevan.org

AVAILABLE FROM WALLBUILDERS

Please go to www.wallbuilders.com to view our numerous books, DVDs, CDs, and other resources that will help you rediscover the true history of America's moral, religious, and constitutional heritage.

You may also enjoy browsing through the Historic Documents and Historic Writings section in the "Library" at www.wallbuilders.com to see the Founders own writings!

800-873-2845　　●　　WWW.WALLBUILDERS.COM

TRANSFORMATIONAL PUBLICATIONS